Profiles of Play

also by Saralea E. Chazan

Simultaneous Treatment of Parent and Child
Second Edition
Saralea E. Chazan
ISBN 1 84310 736 8

of related interest

The Story So Far
Play Therapy Narratives
Edited by Ann Cattanach
ISBN 1 84310 063 0

Amy Elizabeth Goes to Play Therapy
A book to Assist Psychotherapists in Helping Young Children
Understand and Benefit from Play Therapy
Kathleen A. Chara and Paul J. Chara, Jr.
Illustrated by J.M. Berns
ISBN 1 84310 775 9

Children's Stories in Play Therapy
Ann Cattanach
ISBN 1 85302 362 0

Play Therapy
Where the Sky Meets the Underworld
Ann Cattanach
ISBN 1 85302 211 X

Play Therapy with Abused Children
Ann Cattanach
ISBN 1 85302 193 8

Case Studies in Non-directive Play Therapy
Virginia Ryan and Kate Wilson
ISBN 1 85302 912 2

Introduction to Developmental Playtherapy
Playing and Health – Persephone's Journey
Sue Jennings
ISBN 1 85302 635 2

Helping Children to Build Self-Esteem
A Photocopiable Activities Book
Deborah Plummer
ISBN 1 85302 927 0

Profiles of Play

Assessing and Observing Structure and Process in Play Therapy

Saralea E. Chazan

Jessica Kingsley Publishers
London and Philadelphia

First published in the United Kingdom in 2002
by Jessica Kingsley Publishers
116 Pentonville Road
London N1 9JB, UK
and
400 Market Street, Suite 400
Philadelphia, PA 19106, USA

www.jkp.com

Printed digitally since 2005

Library of Congress Cataloging in Publication Data
A CIP catalog record for this book is available from the Library of Congress

British Library Cataloguing in Publication Data
A CIP catalogue record for this book is available from the British Library

ISBN-13: 978 1 84310 703 1
ISBN-10: 1 84310 703 1

For Bob

Contents

Acknowledgments

First and foremost I appreciate the leadership efforts of Paulina Kernberg and the collaboration of Lina Normandin in working to create the *Children's Play Therapy Instrument*. We worked together as a research group at the New York Presbyterian Hospital/Weill Cornell Medical Center, Westchester Division. Working on the CPTI was a creative group effort that impacted constructively upon my effectiveness as a clinician, researcher and teacher. This book is an independent effort on my part to demonstrate the many ways I found this instrument to be helpful in my clinical work. I am grateful to have had this opportunity for professional growth and hope this book will extend what I have learned to others.

There were several other individuals who participated in the early stages of thinking about writing a measure for assessing play activity. Elsa Blum, Alice Frankel, Robert Kruger, and Hannah Scholl were members of the original research group. To establish reliability for the CPTI, three experienced clinicians were recruited from the community—Pauline Jordan, Judith Moskowitz, and Risa Ryger. Their enthusiasm and good will convinced me that in fact the scale could be useful and generate new understandings about the structure and meaning of play activity in psychotherapy. Through their generous donation of time, the scale took on aliveness and reality.

Many colleagues, friends, and students endured listening to me describe the benefits of the scale. Four of them are acknowledged as contributing cases to this book—Eileen Harbader (Carla), Pauline Jordan (Ben), Andrea Salemanto (Kate), and Jonathan Wolf (George). Other supportive individuals included: Caroline Boettcher, Hillary Meyers, Joseph De More, Leslie Jacobs, Catherine Mandelovitch, Jennifer Roberts, Amy Sommer, and Chase Stoball. Many thanks to Marjorie Bresner, Judith Eisenbach, Judith Lobel, Elaine Seitz, and Ava Siegler for reading parts of the manuscript and giving me valuable feedback. The clinical psychology program at New York University welcomed me at a brown bag lunch to discuss the scale with its students. The Institute for Child, Adolescent and Family Psychotherapy enabled me to share some of this material with its students. The Jewish Board of Children and Family Services of New York invited me to rate the play activity of their therapeutic play groups. All of these interactions were valuable contributions to my work.

Several of the case studies were previously published in other versions. Anne was described in the article "Some Comments on the Treatment of Borderline Children" (1989), in R. Fine (ed.) *Current and Historical Perspectives on the Borderline Patient* New York: Brunner/Mazel. The article "Toward a Nonverbal Syntax of Play Therapy" (2001), *Psychoanalytic Inquiry 21, 3*, 394–406 contained some of the material about Carla's treatment. Sammy's complete treatment was described in detail in *Simultaneous Treatment of Parent and Child* (1995) New York: Basic Books. A research presentation of his case material appeared as an article Using the Children's Play Therapy Instrument to measure the development of play in simultaneous treatment (2000), *Infant Mental Health Journal 21, 3, 211–221*.

Completing this book would never have been possible without the encouragement of those closest to the endeavor. Nina Gunzenhauser-Hart agreed to edit the manuscript and was enormously helpful in many ways. Our family currently spans four generations from my mother Ethel Engel, through our children, Daniel and Ronit, Michael and Michelle, Rachel and Daniel, to our grandchildren, Gabriel, Nathan, and Jonah. We all share the joy of playing together and joining together to participate in each other's interests and work. Writing this book emerged in no small part from this shared family experience. My partner in life has been Robert Chazan and in dedicating this book to him I once more acknowledge my gratitude for his continued sustaining faith in my work.

Preface

...play is in fact neither a matter of inner psychic reality nor a matter of external reality...if play is neither inside nor outside, where is it? (Winnicott 1971, p.96).

D. W. Winnicott focuses our attention on the sphere containing play activity, the spatial realm where play takes place. This space or background for playing is both illusory and real. It begins in the interaction between parent and child. It develops further as the child hatches out of the parent–child matrix, now containing within himself the elements for playing. Playing, at this point of separateness, becomes not only an expression of one's individuality but also an extension of the original parent–child relationship. Thus, play activity exists as an interpsychic and intrapsychic mix, a careful balancing of relationships that remain potentially activated and energizing.

How can we communicate in discrete, measurable units about this illusory, yet very real, activity of playing? Play activity is the essence of child psychotherapy. It is synonymous with ongoing therapeutic transactions between therapist and child patient. It is the child's personal and shared vocabulary for describing subjective experience, the experience of doing and not-doing, being and not-being in the presence of another. Playing in therapy is a spontaneous expression. It stretches the confines of everyday reality to the boundaries of make-believe. The impossible transforms to the infinitely possible; private experience is shared with another. How can we capture the complexity of this essential therapeutic process?

The purpose of this book is to provide a language for child therapists, to assist them in specifying what occurs within therapy sessions with their patients. Categorization is essential to this effort but does not imply polarization, exclusion, or simplification. Psychotherapy with children is a complex, dynamic process. It cannot be reduced to simple categories. Overlapping levels of analysis, overdetermined causation, and multiple levels of meaning are the rule. Despite this inherent complexity, however, description of events does require units of observation for clarity and comparison of data. When observations to be collected are specified, data can be juxtaposed in various ways, like pieces in a puzzle, to yield new meaning.

The field of psychology has been profoundly enriched by the intimate linkage between theory and practice. Sigmund Freud, the founder of psychoanalysis, was both a researcher and a clinician. Freud's research deeply influenced his clinical practice, and his experience with patients posed critical questions for his theorizing, stimulating many of the theses he developed about the human psyche. The combination that worked so well for Freud has become generally accepted into the field of clinical psychology, with laboratory enriching the treatment room and vice versa. *Profiles of Play* attempts to follow this paradigm of linking theory with practice. It provides the practitioner with a broad conceptual framework that emphasizes a psychodynamic understanding of child development and the ideas of psychic conflict and defense drawn from ego psychology. Because of its synthetic orientation, however, ideas are included that are derived from behavioral science, cognitive-behavioral formulations, and attachment theory as well. It is anticipated that because of the inclusive nature of this approach to play activity there will be material appropriate for clinician/researchers from a variety of theoretical frameworks.

Profiles of Play emerged from my experience using the *Children's Play Therapy Instrument* (CPTI) as clinician, supervisor, teacher, and researcher. The scale was the result of a lengthy research project on the measurement of children's play in psychotherapy. This project involved researchers who were, at the same time, clinicians. As is so often the case, practice illuminated research and research vivified practice. While the impact of practice on the construction of the CPTI constitutes an interesting story in its own right (Kernberg, Chazan, and Normandin 1998), the focus of this book is upon the usefulness of research for the clinical practice of the child clinician. The assertion is a simple one: Awareness of the categories developed for scientifically measuring children's play bears the potential for enhancing clinical

work. The child psychologist who absorbs the central ideas of the CPTI
will develop useful sensitivity to key aspects of children's play. With this
knowledge she will be able to structure her work more effectively and
monitor the progress of her patients more intelligently. While not fully
trained to utilize the children's play scale scientifically, the attentive reader
will gain valuable new insight from immersing herself in the technicalities
of the scale. The dimensions of this insight will be illustrated by a series of
case studies that show precisely how clinical practice can be informed by
careful scientific research.[1]

It is hoped the reader will be intrigued by this work and consider the
use of these parameters to describe play activity. The utility of having a
method of analysis with which to articulate treatment process, as well as the
attributes of the playing child that interact to produce play activity, is indis-
pensable to the practicing clinician-researcher. The apparent simplicity of
play activity disguises its underlying complex structure. The author's goal
is to expose play activity in child treatment to close scrutiny in order to
better understand the meaning of the experience for the playing child.

The central hypothesis of this book is that patterns of play activity can
be identified by observing children while at play. These patterns articulate
the relative contribution of the various parameters that combine to produce
play activity. The patterns, or profiles, of play activity reflect a specific
child's experience of himself and others while playing, as well as his strategies for coping and adaptation.

The introductory chapter explores more fully the importance of play
activity for child psychotherapy. Contrasting descriptions of three children
are given to illustrate differences between a child's expected play activity
and play activity suggestive of the need to intervene. The first steps in
analyzing play activity in the therapy session are then described, including
pre-play activity, play activity, non-play activity, and interruptions. When
the units of play activity have been identified, one such unit is selected for
further analysis. The first level of analysis, *descriptive analysis*, includes the

---

1   Generally therapists will be referred to in the feminine gender, while
     child patients will be referred to in the masculine gender. Exceptions
     occur in the description of actual clinical cases.

more overt characteristics of the play activity, and who participated in it and how.

Chapter 1 describes the next level of analysis of the play activity, *structural analysis*. The case of Ben, a three-and-a-half-year-old child referred for consultation because of aggressive behavior at home and in daycare, is used to illustrate. The therapist's process notes of Ben's session are analyzed into a profile of segments indicating the child's movement in and out of play activity, and the processes underlying play activity are measured using four major scales: affective components, cognitive components, narrative components, and developmental components.

Chapters 2 to 5 introduce the analysis of coping–defensive strategies observable in a child's play activity. These coping–defensive strategies are arranged along a continuum of four clusters: adaptive, conflicted, polarized/rigid, and extremely anxious/isolated. In the CPTI, these clusters were originally named to correspond to the continuum of diagnostic categories: normal, neurotic, borderline, and psychotic. In this book, however, the descriptors for the clusters of play strategies have been changed. This change in naming the clusters was introduced to make them appropriately descriptive of play activity and not synonymous with pathology. They were chosen to emphasize the quality, style, and focus of the play activity, not to be isomorphic with a diagnosis of the child's mental health.

Chapter 2 highlights the playing style of the *adaptive player*, as defined by a relative predominance of adaptive coping–defensive strategies in the play activity. Two cases are introduced, those of four-and-a-half-year-old Carla and nine-year-old Kate. Carla is able to retrieve early nonverbal experience through play activity, expanding earlier rigid punitive play themes. Kate creates a wishful world of fantasy that uses humor to offset disappointments in the everyday world.

Chapter 3 presents almost six-year-old George, a *conflicted player*, who begins treatment as a child preoccupied with his own thoughts and distant from his therapist. As interaction increases between the two participants in play, George's conflicts become more apparent. He is torn between mischief and compliance. Through make-believe he is able to openly express his ambivalent feelings without fear of retaliation. This is a relatively brief treatment that results in gains in both behavior and playfulness, although an approach-avoidant conflict remains a major characteristic of the play. Most important, George is able to share his state of loneliness with his therapist and depict it in the creation of an imaginary planet.

Chapter 4 describes two very different young girls, *rigid/polarized players*, whose defensive strategies deeply restrict their capacity to play. Rebecca is a shy, constricted, inhibited child who begins her treatment at age six and ends at age eight. She longs to be a novelist, but cannot express herself in writing. She tentatively at first, and then with increasing fervor begins to play out her wishes and fears. Colorful, outgoing characters emerge that fill the space once occupied by a rigid and frightened child. Anna, also six years old, enters treatment an aggressive and oppositional child. Her play activity is interrupted by fierce disruptive outbursts of destructive impulses. Over a three-year course of treatment, she gradually gains control over her polarized states of "goodness" and "badness" and these opposite feeling states no longer threaten her creativity in play.

Chapter 5 introduces Sammy, a child who entered treatment at age two years, four months, an *extremely anxious/isolated player.* Nine months of treatment were recorded on videotape. Sessions from the beginning and end of treatment were rated by two independent raters, originally trained for participation in the reliability study of the CPTI (Chazan 2000). Profiles based on ratings of the level of segmentation, as well as the shift in coping–defensive strategies are presented, documenting change over time. Since Sammy is a very young child, he and his mother are seen in simultaneous treatment. The mother has her own individual sessions with the therapist, and also participates in dyadic sessions with her child. These dyadic sessions are described with a dual focus, Sammy's increasing capacity to play and changes reflected in the mother–child relationship.

Chapter 6 focuses on the role of play activity in the overall development of the child. The child's awareness of himself as playing is viewed as a measure of his awareness of being in the state of pretending. This mental state of pretense is explored as a forerunner to the child's capacity to become cognizant of perspectives other than his own. Revisiting three of the clinical cases presented earlier in the book, the author traces how for each of these three children a shift in the profile of coping–defensive strategies accompanies these important developments in self-awareness.

It is important to make clear that the concept of profiling is used to describe a method of capturing the individuality in a child's style of playing. The complexity of the process of being at play has always made it elusive and difficult to identify. What is seen as simply playing is in fact a unique mental state, a unique set of attributes, and a unique perspective. It must be emphasized that the use of the concept of profiling is not to create a set of stereotypes in which to rigidly categorize children. On the contrary, these categories of playing contain many different variables describing levels of relationship, levels of cognitive and affective development, as well as capacity for creating narrative. The reader will come to recognize that styles of play activity are not necessarily synonymous with behavior or overall emotional well-being. Rather, it is the unique state of playing that permits the full expression of a child's individuality to emerge. The function of these play profiles is to capture the essence of play activity in all its complexity.

For whom is this book written? Certainly child clinicians, including therapists and practitioners who focus on treatment issues, as well as their students preparing to enter the field. Clinicians working with adults might also find this approach to play activity useful in understanding their patients. Academicians studying child development will find the definitions of play activity relevant to their work. Although not written from a research perspective, many of the formulations contained in this volume can be applied to formal scientific studies. Social workers, speech and language therapists, pediatric nurses, child development workers, pediatricians, and teachers are all professionals with allied interests who can gain insights by observing play from a new viewpoint. Finally, parents who are involved with and vitally interested in the development of their children can learn much about the unique role of play activity in the lives of their children. With this enhanced understanding they can gain a greater appreciation for their own important contribution to play activity, a contribution that usually goes unacknowledged.

Introduction
Observing Play Activity

I can tell the story of my child's play.
I can read it without words
From the sounds that resonate within me,
The sounds of laughter—the sounds of joy.

Johnny is just four years old. His mother notices him one day closing and opening the swinging door to the kitchen. It is a bright sunny day, and light is streaming in through the windows. Mother wonders why he doesn't stop the racket and come and join her in the kitchen. Anyhow, he might even catch his fingers in the door! As she approaches, she stops as she hears him saying, "Hi! Do you want to play?" Mother looks around her, certain—or almost certain—that no one else is about in the house. Slam. There it goes again! What is going on? She decides to approach slowly.

The hall is narrow, and Johnny does not see her. As she continues to observe, the meaning of Johnny's actions becomes clear. As he opens the door, the light from the window projects his shadow on the floor. When he closes the door—slams the door—the image is gone! Johnny is heard to call, "Bye, bye!" And then he opens the door and the process is repeated. Mother is amazed. Although Johnny has had a fantasy friend, that friend has always existed in imagination only. Here is the friendly image appearing at Johnny's behest! Or is Johnny aware it was his own shadow? Mother decides not to intrude, but to keep a watchful eye on this intriguing dialogue.

Jane is entering kindergarten this fall. She generally enjoys activities on the playground and going to friends" houses for play dates. In addition to social activities, Jane enjoys quiet solitary time, and she tends to seek it out after a busy morning in preschool. Jane does not want to play with anyone else; she clearly wants to be alone, although she takes comfort with the presence of her mother or the housekeeper elsewhere in the house. This afternoon, Jane has set up a school scene with her miniature figures. She spends considerable time arranging the tiny furniture into a doll corner, a block corner, and a place for sharing experiences and listening to stories.

Jane is busy and involved with her play. She begins to speak for the different characters. There are three girls involved in playing house; a boy joins them to be the father. Another child is building blocks. First he builds a tall tower and then a train station. As his play becomes noisier, another child comes and grabs a block from him. The teacher intervenes. A mother arrives with her daughter, who is crying; she does not want to stay alone in school. Jane does not know what to do this time. The toy child cries louder and louder. The other toy children turn to watch. Some of them begin to cry, too. Jane goes off to find her mother. She cannot continue to play alone.

Tom is eleven years old. His parents have finally arranged to have the basketball hoop hung up over the garage door. It seemed forever until the carpenter could come. But now it is ready! Tom runs to find his ball. "Yup! There it is!" Thump, thump, thump goes the ball on the pavement as Tom reaches back for a sure shot, and then—he'll try again. The afternoon becomes evening, but Tom doesn't notice. It's time for dinner. But Tom doesn't notice. His parents are amazed at his persistence. Tom tries his lay-up, then he tries a jump shot and a dunk. He feels his body jump and his feet pound the pavement. He speaks in quiet tones to intimate comrades and fans, of whom others are unaware. Just in time for supper, the buzzer sounds. And Tom does notice. As the crowd cheers, he knows they notice, too, and are proud of his grand achievements!

Principles of Play

The three children described were all engrossed in play activity. What do these activities have in common? Can shared principles of play be discerned in their behavior?

Play is first and foremost playful. Play occupies a realm outside of everyday events. It has to do with imaginings and trial action. Anything is possible, and no consequences need intrude. Outcome is open-ended and up for grabs. Play can be infinite or finite, depending on the whim of the player(s); play is active, not static. It emerges as part of the movement of actions and ideas across space and time.

Play activity is of crucial importance to children of all ages. It provides a context for social relationships and spontaneous learning. It can follow sets of rules, private or shared. Play activity is characteristic of living and life. It is both regressive and progressive. It provides a medium for the growth of a sense of self, competence, and confidence in the surrounding world.

Play is recognized by its focused attention. All three of our players are absorbed in their activity. This attention provides the framework within which the play activity emerges. The quality of this absorbed attention is palpable. The attentive state seems to arise from within the child and transport him to a different sphere—a place of possibilities. The quality of this unusual absorption informs us that this activity is important. In fact, the activity at that moment seems to define the child himself.

Play is also recognized by its expressiveness. It is a universal language of communication. The major avenues for expression are feelings overtly expressed and feeling states shared. The concentration informs us of the importance of these messages, often nonverbal and universal in their appeal. Human feelings are the basic data generated by play activity, and play activity cannot exist without the expression of feelings. Feelings expressed can range from terror to infatuation. Modulation and regulation of these feeling states are necessary to assure continuity of the play activity. If outbursts occur, there is potential for the disruption of the focused state that maintains play activity. Within the sphere of play activity, feelings can be fully expressed, as they are severed from consequences that might be encountered in the everyday world.

Initiation of play activity may be signaled by the child with the direct invitation "Let's play!", or by a spontaneous smile, or the expression of glee, surprise, anxiety, or fear that shows something important is occurring. In initiating play, the child is clearly representing an aspect of his world. He is conveying an aspect of his experience and how he organizes this experience. Thus, Johnny is showing us the anticipation of the appearance of his shadow. He is telling us to watch with him and witness the emergence of the shadow image he anticipates. We learn from his play that he can begin to construct the image of a partner and hold it in mind, even though the fantasy partner is not there to be seen. This capacity to hold images in memory is an important developmental advance. Tom clearly has the image of successfully landing the ball in the basket. His anticipation of success accounts for his persistence.

Play activity can also be a measure of developmental advance. The child uses objects in a symbolic way to represent other objects that are not available. Parents are often chagrined to find their children inventing toys from ordinary objects in preference to expensive store-bought toys. Jane's use of small objects gives her a sense of control over events in her mini-world. As language develops, it makes possible the narration of events. Jane is able to tell the story unfolding in her play activity and speak for each of the characters represented. Now the child is able to encompass past and future in his play, as well as to share the many possible outcomes of his imaginings. Make-believe becomes a recognized arena for play activity, extending the present moment to magical imaginary realms.

It is difficult for a parent to recall the antecedents of this elaborated narrative play activity. It has evolved as the direct descendant of the baby's concentrated gaze at his caregiver's features, the sound of her voice, and his first sights of the physical surroundings. Slowly, play activity has come to engage the various functions of the child's thinking, talking, imagining, and interaction with others. As development progresses, play activity differentiates in its various forms to contain cultural meanings and increasingly abstract forms of expression. Play activity, then, should not be underestimated. It is the human equivalent of infinity and the hope for tomorrow.

Play Activity and the Representational World of the Child

Earliest representations begin as subjective experiences within the dyadic relationship of caregiver and child. Daniel Stern (1985) calls these repetitive experiences of self in the presence of a self-regulating other "Representations of Interactions that have been Generalized" (RIGs). Memories of having been with the caregiver are available to the child whenever an attribute of the RIG is present. When different memories of being with a caregiver are activated, Stern suggests, different RIGs are activated and the child reexperiences the many ways of being with this caregiver. In the case of both caregivers who are present and those who are absent, the child must deal with the complete array of experiences, or history, of being with this self-regulatory other.

Stern describes the activation of the subjective experience of being with a historical self-regulating other as an encounter with an evoked companion. This evoked companion emerges from the RIG, a generalized representation of the interaction with the self-regulating other, not as the recollection of an actual happening but as "an active exemplar of such happenings." RIGs are continuously updated by new experiences occurring as the child interacts with significant others. As with John Bowlby's (1969) internal working models, RIGs tend to be conservative. The more past experience is built up and consolidated, the less impact any one single event will have. If the child is actually alone, the current experience in the here and now can include the memory (in or out of awareness) of having been with another. The RIG can be conceptualized as the basic building block from which Bowlby's working models are constructed. Like working models, RIGs represent accumulated past experience and serve a guiding function in creating expectations for the present and future. Similar conceptualizations of how early representations are formed out of social interactions include merger experiences (Mahler 1968), self-objects (Kohut 1971), early forms of internalization (Kernberg 1975; Sandler & Sandler 1978), and the origins of self-object experiences (Beebe & Lachman 1988).

A child at play is invested in his own representational world. As D. W. Winnicott (1971) noted, play is an active process that occurs in a "play space," the overlapping spheres of two persons at play. The first such space may be the caregiver's lap. Gradually, play space expands and loses its sense of physicality. The floor becomes the terra firma supporting the playing child, and time contains the actions of the play. Time may be experienced as "timeless" as the child becomes absorbed by play. Past and future become condensed in the present moment, as memories are evoked by the play activity. Joseph Sandler and Bernard Rosenblatt (1962) stressed that the crucial factors determining the child's play activity flow from his cumulative relationship history, rather than from an isolated event, behavior, or personality characteristic. Thus, if a child can distill from his experiences with others a zest for inquiry, a curiosity about the unusual, a confidence in his world as a safe place, these experiences hold the promise of rich and diverse play activity (Moran 1987; Neubauer 1987).

Erik and Joan Erikson (1972) studied play structures of children who were given the instructions to "build something" and then to "tell a story." Following ten to twenty minutes of play, each child presented a structure characterized by a unique style of representation. Observing these same children over time, the Ericksons recorded impressive variation as well as continuity among play themes. Thirty years later these same play constructions, or representational worlds, could be discerned as condensed statements of a theme to become prominent in the child's later life. Although some themes were repetitive, as seen in "working through" a traumatic experience, other themes reflected playful renewal. Play themes served functions of both confession and communication; the Eriksons stressed, however, that play activity also served the joy of self-expression. Play activities exercised growing abilities, as well as helping to master complex life situations.

The Eriksons valued all of these variations in play representations equally. They described play activity as depending upon an interplay of the child's inner resources with the nature of the task. In their view, play activity connotes freedom within prescribed limits. Whenever either the freedom or the limits are withdrawn, the play activity ends.

The Role of Play Activity in Child Psychotherapy

Play activity has been widely acknowledged as ubiquitous to child treatment. Indeed, when a child is unable to play, that inability is understood by others as an indication of his distress. What characteristics of play activity make it intrinsic to the process of psychic recovery and repair?

Creativity, as experienced while playing, comes alive as a dialectic between the past and future, experienced in the present moment. It occurs in a middle ground between the impossible and the probable. In play, disbelief is suspended and belief is extended to include the imagined or conjured reality. For children who suffer the pain of trauma, disappointment, and untimely disillusionment, the opportunity to play is a chance to revise and transform the effects of the past. The greater the trauma, the more overwhelming and powerful are the intruding disabling feelings and images. In many instances, perception of the possibility for change may occur only as the child becomes aware of himself as a player, playing in relationship to others. Thus, the evolution of play activity proceeds in tandem with the development of separation–individuation processes and the growth of the self (Mahler, Pine, & Bergman 1975).

Play activity in child treatment undergoes a process of change that in many ways parallels the process of development experienced in the normal course of a child's growth. Play activity is sensory, perceptual, and potentially symbolic. Through its use of symbols play activity is extended into the sphere of representational thought and abstract elaboration. In treatment, play activity facilitates the modification of past experiences and the innovation of new coping strategies. During treatment, changes in the child's play activity transform his perspective on significant relationships and alter his adaptation to his surroundings.

In the treatment of very young children and more disturbed children, the emphasis in therapy is upon facilitating the discovery of meaning, rather than uncovering the hidden meaning in their play (Slade 1994). Thus, the therapist cannot understand the meaning of play activity without the child's active participation. Meaning is not an a priori presupposition imposed on play activity. Rather, meaning is an attribute of play activity emerging out of shared moments of subjective experience. Before the play becomes truly representational, the therapist plays alongside the child to make sense of things. Experiences are labeled and linked together. Tangles of feelings and impulses are unraveled. By means of such play these children discover what they feel, what they know, and what they want. Enacting experiences and feelings in play, rather than speaking words alone, the child creates structure. By playing with the child, the therapist becomes a part of the discovery of what the child means to say and means to feel.

Arietta Slade cautioned that it is only when experience can be known and represented in activity that it can be hidden, and we can then interpret the symbols as having hidden meaning. Once representational structures are in place, wishes can be disguised and the assumption be made that the symbols available to consciousness are linked to unconscious processes. For example, we do not understand why Johnny is opening and shutting the door until he verbalizes, "Hi! Do you want to play?" We then can understand the meaning of his actions as a prelude to a fantasy of shared activity.

The profiles, or configurations, of play activity reflect a specific child's experience of himself and others, as well as his strategies for coping and adaptation. Do the profiles of play activity of children in treatment differ from those whose behavior has not suggested the need for treatment? The answer to this query is both yes and no; rather than being a categorical distinction, the difference observed is usually a matter of degree. To illustrate let's revisit Johnny, Jane, and Tom and imagine what their play activity might be like if it were cause for concern and they were referred for professional consultation.

Four-year-old Johnny is a door slammer. It began insidiously about six months ago. Whenever he passes an open door, he must slam it shut. If it is not latched shut, he will work at opening it again and closing it again. If left to his own devices, he will continue this behavior until forcefully told to stop. Compliance is an issue for Johnny, and he does not seem to listen. Rather, he is absorbed by the activity of closing and shutting objects. Sometimes it is not a door but a drawer or a box. Johnny seems transfixed by this activity, as if in a trance. It is usually repetitive, with no variation in movement or any verbal communication. Johnny's mother watches this activity perplexed. At first she thought he was playing, but it is an odd repetitive play, with a monotonous tone. When she tries to interrupt his play, he ignores her. She feels hurt by this rejection and tends to withdraw rather than intervene. When she does have to put a stop to it, she becomes infuriated. Recently, she has come to feel increasingly distant from Johnny, and this estrangement alarms her. Although he is eating and sleeping well, she decides to seek a consultation regarding this strange play behavior.

Although Johnny's behavior here bears a resemblance to the activity in the first vignette, the communication to the observer is vastly different in these two scenes. In the first instance, Johnny is not alone. He has conjured a playmate who comes and goes at his initiative. Johnny need not feel lonely in this play; he can always welcome in his fantasy friend to play. Mother is reassured by his immersion and even smiles in recognition, as she can understand the fun of having a guest appear at your behest. In the second instance, there is little communication in the act of playing. Johnny seems self-absorbed in a repetitive act that has little meaning. His play does nothing to further human connectedness and leaves mother feeling rejected, while he is impervious to his surroundings. In treatment this same repetitive behavior would reappear, and the therapist would need to test the limits of his rigid play stance. Would they pervade the entire session, or could he be distracted in some way? Would he become more lively in inter-action, given appropriate support?

> Five-year-old Jane will not play alone. Although she can play with her toys and dolls in an age-appropriate manner, she always needs her mother to participate. Unlike Jane in the first vignette, who can play alone if an empathic caregiver is available, Jane clings to her caregiver and will not relinquish her for an instant. Mother often feels trapped by her daughter's demandingness, although she is intrigued by the doll play that ensues. Mother worries that perhaps she has "spoiled" her daughter with too much attention. What can she do to become free of this entanglement? Mother feels Jane should be sufficiently inter-ested in her own playing and should not need her to make the play complete. Most upsetting, when mother refuses to play with her, Jane refuses to play at all.

The two vignettes are strikingly different. Jane in the first instance is capable of playing alone in the presence of another, and even in the proximate presence of the other, not immediately present in the room. In the other instance, play activity ceases without the immediate presence and involvement of the caregiver. Although the level of play remains consistent, it is not consistently available to the child in the second instance. Her need for the presence of the other is unremitting. The difference in social level of development in these two vignettes results in two different profiles of play activity. In the second instance, psychotherapy is indicated to assist the dyad towards separation and the child towards individuation.

> Tom's parents eagerly await the arrival of the basketball hoop. Tom's father remembers having his own basketball hoop over the garage door when he was a boy. He spent endless hours of fun, shared with friends in the neighborhood, throwing balls and shooting baskets. His antici-pation is great as he envisions his son's delight. He arranges to mount the basket in time for Tom's eleventh birthday. Much to his parents' astonishment, Tom is at first very excited and then walks away from the basket as though it were not there. Several weeks later Tom is still not using the hoop. He sits and stares at it sometimes, as though making a careful plan of approach, but never begins to play. When his friends come over, they play, but Tom sits on the sideline. Tom's parents are puzzled: Is Tom discouraged, intimidated, not interested? In their per-plexity they cannot figure out why Tom will not play. It only makes matters worse when they try to intervene. They decide to seek profes-sional assistance.

In the second vignette, Tom is acting to negate the fun of playing ball. His play profile is vastly different from the active initiative he takes towards mastery in the first vignette. The two different patterns of play activity suggest two very different family contexts. In the second instance, the con-straints placed by the child on play activity suggest a need for consultation.

Identifying Play Activity: Segmentation

Play activity is an ongoing component of all creative life processes. At times it is the dominant and sole component; at other times it serves a background function, providing a context for other kinds of activity; and at still other times it is a barely discernible element within the context of a larger activity.

Segmentation is the process of sorting out a child's activity into categories. Identifying shared commonalities among child behaviors enables the observer to begin to arrange and label his observations. Establishing a nomenclature is always a combination of arbitrary and subjective decisions. However, it is a first step towards isolating the aspect of a child's activity the observer seeks to understand. In order to study play activity the observer must be able to consistently identify play activity and share his criteria with others also observing the playing child. When agreement is attained the observer choosing to study play activity can focus on play activity itself, its duration, content, and function. All further analyses of play activity depend upon this first step of segmentation.

Can play activity be distinguished from non-play activity? What are the attributes specific to play activity? In the manual of the Children's Play Therapy Instrument (CPTI) (Kernberg, Chazan, & Normandin 1997) the attributes of play activity versus non-play activity are used to define discrete segments of a child's activity. These segments can then be sequentially ordered over time to render a quantitative representation of the progression of a child's ongoing activity. This categorical analysis enables the observer to compare segments of predominantly play activity with segments identified as predominantly non-play activity. It also provides a profile of the overall progression and flow of child activity within the therapeutic hour. In order to be classified as an independent segment, the child's activity (play, pre-play, non-play, interruption) must last at least 20 seconds.

Play Activity

Play activity is identified by the absorption of the child in what he is doing. There are several behavioral markers that are characteristic attributes of play activity. Play activity is often accompanied by a verbalization of intent, such as "Let's play." For example, four-year-old Johnny invites his phantom friend to join him in playing. "Hi! Do you want to play?" is his invitation to his partner in fantasy who will join him in playing. Although the shadowy friend comes and goes, he supplies the social component necessary to sustain Johnny's play.

On the other hand, Jane is playing alone (although she is aware a caring adult is also at home). She is involved in solitary play with a group of fantasy characters; she is the director of their actions. She takes the initiative to define roles for the different characters: mother, father, three children, and teacher. Jane does more than just assign roles and activate the characters; she also devises a script for the play. Jane's fantasy narrative has a beginning, a middle, and an end.

What if a child does not extend an invitation to play or create a play scene? Are there other markers of play activity?

Tom is very engrossed in his ball playing. As mentioned above this purposeful concentration is an important attribute of play activity. He also expresses pleasure and delight in his activity, another marker of play. The specific feelings expressed may vary from positive glee, surprise, and fun to negative anxiety or fear. Some children are curious about the threat posed by danger. Their focus on a specific activity and their purposeful use of toy objects are both indications of play activity.

Play activity is infinitely variable and is identifiable by the nonverbal attributes of focused concentration, purposeful choice of a toy or object, and specific affective expression. It may be introduced with a verbal invitation and elaborated to contain role representations and narration of a story of play events. At times the role representations and narrative may be communicated through actions (mime), liberating play activity from the constraints of verbalization. All of the attributes of play activity may be present, or only one attribute of play activity may be present. Regardless of the number of attributes observed, any one or more of the above attributes indicates the presence of play activity.

Pre-Play Activity

It is often discernible that a child is preparing or "setting the stage" for play activity. For instance, a child may pick up a toy, begin to explore it, manipulate it, or give it symbolic meaning. Sometimes a child does not proceed into the play activity itself but spends the entire therapy session in preparation. In other instances, a child may be fully engrossed in the activities of sorting, aligning, and constructing, which become the play activity, rather than preparation for more elaborate play. Oftentimes pre-play can only be discerned by reviewing the play session in its entirety. Pre-play may occur not only at the beginning of a segment of play activity but embedded within the context of continuing play. For example, the child pauses, chooses a new toy, or focuses upon the therapist in the midst of his play activity.

Non-Play Activity

Non-play activity includes all behaviors outside pre-play and play activity: eating, reading, doing homework, conversing with the therapist. He may be talking about doing something, recounting an event, or planning an activity, all with a serious demeanor. In all of these activities, whether the child is compliant or negativistic, he is involved in routine duties or work defined by an outside agent. Absent are the qualities of investment of self for the sake of doing the activity, pursuing a task simply for the delight of trying, asking a question primarily in the search for self-expression and personal meaning.

Non-play is the realm of daily events, the ongoing everyday processing of information and the performance of necessary tasks, "fitting in" or not "fitting in." In the therapy session, many non-play activities lead effortlessly to play activities, and the reverse is true as well. What is bridged is a space between two realms, at times obvious, at other times hidden by human subtleties. Essential to the effectiveness of the therapy session is the awareness of the therapist of when this bridge has been crossed, and how—precipitously, carefully, with wonder, or with disdain. At these junctures the therapist is receiving crucial communication about the child and his subjective experience of how he views himself and his creativity, as well as his perception of others and how they perceive him. Are they open to all aspects of his existence, or is there a rigid line drawn between what may be experienced—what may be recognized and shared—and what must remain hidden without awareness?

Interruptions

Interruptions occur within the session whenever a child leaves the room and cannot continue his activity within the session. Interruptions can occur during play or non-play activity, for example when the child needs to go to the bathroom or must reconnoiter with his caregiver in the waiting room. These behaviors usually reflect some mounting tension within the session that cannot be tolerated by the child, so that he seeks release by leaving the room. Often an apprehensive child toward the end of a session will need to check on his parents' whereabouts. At times it is a particular content within the session that is contributing to mounting tensions and causes the child to flee. The therapist needs to heed these interrupting behaviors as a signal of subjective distress.

Descriptive Analysis of Play Activity

Once the therapy session has been segmented, the segments identified as play activity can be studied in detail. When the Child Play Therapy Instrument (CPTI, Kernberg, Chazan, & Normandin 1997) is applied, the longest segment of play activity is usually selected for study, but the method of analysis can be applied to any segment of the play activity.

The analysis begins with a description of the overt behavior in the play activity—the type of play activity entered into, who initiates the play, how it progresses (or fails to progress), how it ends, and the sphere in which it takes place.

Categories of Play Activity

The Children's Play Therapy Instrument classifies types of play activity into several categories. These categories may overlap; they are not necessarily mutually exclusive. Generally play activity is assigned to the most advanced category.

Sensory Activity

The activity is based on the sensory quality of the object, such as texture. For example, the child caresses the binding on the edge of a pillow.

Gross Motor Activity

These activities involve large muscles of the body and include jumping, climbing, and throwing a ball.

Exploratory Activity

The child becomes familiar with the various features of a play object. For example, the child explores the contents of a box.

Manipulative Activity

The child manipulates toys, often with the motive of achieving mastery. Examples include putting pegs in holes, stacking blocks, and completing a simple form board.

Sorting-Aligning Activity

Toy objects are sorted or aligned with no further elaboration of symbolic meaning. For example, the child lines up a row of cars.

Cause-Effect Activity

The child produces a specific effect using play materials and makes a connection between two events. For example, the child rolls a ball down a ramp, varying the level of incline of the ramp.

Problem-Solving Activity

In this more advanced level of manipulation, the child might put together train tracks to make a pattern, alternating shapes and sizes of pieces to achieve the desired result.

Construction Activity

The child builds a whole or part of an identifiable object, such as a house or a tower.

Exploring, manipulating, sorting, and aligning objects can be observed as independent categories of play activity or as preparation for more elaborated play. When these activities are preliminary to later elaborated play activity, they are segmented as pre-play activity. An example would be setting up the doll furniture used later in a scene of family interaction. If the activity had ended with the child putting the furniture in different piles, it would be classified as sorting-aligning play activity. Another example would be sorting out blocks of different sizes and shapes. If the activity ends at that point, it would be classified as sorting-aligning play activity. If the blocks are used to construct a house the activity would be classified as construction play activity (the play activity is classified in the highest category). If the block sorting was preliminary to fantasy play (or subsequent fantasy play was implicit to the arrangement), the activity would be segmented as pre-play (preparation for play).

Imitation (Literal) Activity

The child imitates a complete, realistic role, using objects as they are used in the real world. For example, the child says to the therapist, "Here comes the nurse to take the temperature."

Traumatic Activity

The child persists in playing out a specific theme in a repetitive manner. The feelings expressed contain a component of pressure, anxiety, or outright despair and sadness. The play either does not move towards resolution or, if it does, has a bad ending. The play activity may involve the insertion of incongruous activity (for example, eating with daddy on the toilet) or transient accusations at the therapist ("you made me play this," "you want to hurt me").

Fantasy Activity

Objects or persons undergo a transformation and perform activities and functions that are imaginary, confabulated, magical, animistic, or grossly exaggerated. The child requires the use of pretense in order for the play activity to proceed, for example, by assuming the role of Superman.

Game Play Activity

The child plays a structured game with mutually shared rules, such as checkers, *Connect Four*, *Candyland*, or *Monopoly*.

Art Activity

The child engages in drawing, painting, or other art activity for expressive purposes.

A given segment of play activity may combine several categories. For instance, a child may be constructing a castle for a beautiful princess. As much interest is being invested in the activity of construction as in the fantasy attribution of the building. In this case, the child would be demonstrating both construction and fantasy play activity.

In other instances there may be a progression from one category of play activity to another and subsequent return. For example, the child begins to play with blocks, leaves the blocks, and begins fantasy play with some toy figures. He then leaves the toy figures and returns to block play. The sequence of play activities may be meaningful, as may the pattern of progression and regression in the categories of play activity. Thus, one child may be initially interested in the texture and sensory aspects of clay and then suddenly independently animate a clay family, while another child remains fully absorbed in the sensory qualities of the clay for the entire session. Clearly, it is crucial for the therapist to note both the selection of types of play activity and the sequencing of these selections.

A review of these categories of play activity reveals a progression in complexity of play behaviors. It is important to note whether or not the child is using symbolic thought in pursuit of his play activity. Several of these categories, such as fantasy play and game play, lend themselves to symbolic representation, but others, such as imitation play, construction play, and cause-effect play may also have symbolic components. It is important to note these distinctions, which indicate the child's progress from sensory to perceptual to more abstract modes of thought.

Script Description of the Play Activity

After identifying the category or categories of play activity, the therapist examines how the play activity segment progresses from beginning to end. A writer might consider the play activity in terms of the basic questions who? what? when? where? how? Hence, this step is called *script description*. The CPTI analyzes the script of the play activity segment in terms of four formal aspects: *initiation, facilitation, inhibition,* and *ending.* Included under these headings is an analysis of the child's intentions in the play and his contributions to the unfolding of the play activity, as well as the kinds of interactions that occur between therapist and child.

Initiation

Either the child or the adult may initiate the play activity. Is it a spontaneous beginning, or is it marked by delay and hesitation? Do therapist and patient collaborate in beginning the activity, or is one partner active and the other passive?

Facilitation

Is the play activity maintained because of the primary interest of the therapist, of the child, or of both participants? Is there a change in level of participation as the play unfolds? Facilitation may include the following behaviors: giving instructions, telling how the play should continue, giving suggestions, pointing to objects, and suggesting new scenes or themes for the play narrative.

Inhibition

Does interference with the play activity originate with the child, with the adult, or as the result of the combined interaction of the two partners? Inhibition occurs when either the child or the therapist is reluctant to use play materials spontaneously, makes comments that detract from the flow of the play, or expresses a negative attitude.

Ending

The play activity may come to an end because the child is satiated and does not need to continue playing. Whether the ending is abrupt or gradual, the child communicates that he is "satisfied" with his play activity and has had "enough." For example, the child hands the paintbrush to the therapist, saying "All done." Such an ending reflects the child's capacity to regulate his own experience and conceptualize a play event with a beginning, middle, and end. The child can begin to differentiate himself from the play activity and express his sense of completeness.

At the other extreme, the child may disrupt the play with expressions of intense anxiety, anger, or sexualized excitement that end the play. For example, a child may lose control of his aggressive impulses and begin to attack the therapist or destroy toys. The activity and associated feelings are no longer contained within the safety of a play framework.

Alternatively, the child may also indicate his ending of the play indirectly, in a number of ways. He may change the focus of his play to non-play or become distracted by unrelated activities outside the playroom. Many times children do not anticipate an ending to play activity; the ending becomes obvious only after the shift away from play activity has occurred. To identify it, the observer must retrace the child's activity to identify the juncture at which the play activity ended. The child may end the play activity without turning to another organized activity. Rising tensions within himself or within the interaction with the therapist may cause him to interrupt the play by leaving the room, using avoidance to lessen his distress. Or he might shift from play activity to non-play activity such as eating or talking to the therapist.

The play activity may also be ended by the adult in several ways. The therapist may indicate withdrawal by showing a lack of response, interest, or empathy. The therapist may set limits on behavior ("We cannot throw the ball here") or indicate that the session is about to end. The therapist may also interrupt the play activity—by taking a telephone call, for example.

The Spheres of Play Activity

D. W. Winnicott (1971) described the transitional space within which play takes place as a middle realm between the polarities of the real world and fantasy. Within this realm, Erik Erikson (1972) defined three spheres of play activity. In the *autosphere* the child plays with reference to his own body. For instance, the child wriggles his fingers or plays with the beads of his necklace. In the *microsphere* the child plays in a miniature toy world, usually using miniature replicas or substitutes for real objects. In the *macrosphere* the child plays with full-size objects from the real world; he goes beyond the small area delineated for small toys and uses the entire room, or the person of the therapist, such as by examining desk drawers and pockets.

Each of these spheres indicates a different level of relationship to the external world and the degree to which the child needs to control his world in order to engage in play activity. Each sphere differs in the amount of autonomy available to the child. In the autosphere, he is restricted to bodily sensations and needs. The microsphere offers him maximal opportunities for exploration within a small world. In the macrosphere he engages the world as it is and is confronted with his relative smallness and dependence on others. How the child copes and adapts to each of these spheres reflects his individual development and his perspective on himself and his world.

Revisiting Johnny, Jane, and Tom: Descriptive Analysis

The procedures of segmentation and descriptive analysis can be clarified by applying them to the pairs of observations of the three children described earlier in the chapter. The discussion that follows analyzes the two versions of each child's behavior, highlighting the occurrence of play activity, patterns of interaction between players, and the sphere within which play activity takes place. This analysis produces distinctive and sharply contrasting profiles of the child's activity.

Revisiting Johnny

In the initial presentation of Johnny's play activity, Johnny's script has two characters, himself and a fantasy friend. His mother is a watchful observer. He is taking full initiative in beginning the play and facilitating the play. There is no inhibition of the play. We do not know how the play will end. Johnny might reach play satiation, might have enough of the activity and walk away, with mother a silent observer of the play and never intervening. Another scenario might have mother becoming part of the play by taking on the role of the entering friend. Alternatively, she might end the play by setting a limit and asking Johnny to come away from the doorway. Johnny might choose to continue the play away from the doorway, asking his friend to come inside and play. In this last instance there might be some inhibition in the play caused by mother's intervention, but not a complete cessation. In this play activity Johnny has been playing in the macrosphere, with full-sized objects and spaces, a doorway and hallway. If he invites his friend indoors, they might settle down to play with trains, in which case they would be playing in the microsphere. Playing with small toys, Johnny would be choosing to step out of the everyday world into an imaginary world he can more fully control. While his mother felt some consternation at witnessing the fantasy friend possibly taking tangible form in the shape of a shadow, she might feel less concerned about his fantasy play with toys. If Johnny were perceiving the shadow as a reflection of his own body, moving as he moved, then he would be playing in the autosphere, which is centered upon the sensory self. By using language to greet his "visitor," Johnny gives us a clue that this is dyadic play. His partner is not autonomous, however, and depends upon Johnny for all of his actions.

The observer might suppose from these formal features of Joi
play activity that he is an outgoing child, willing to take initiati
interact with others. In fact, Johnny does not like to be alone, and he cr
a twin to follow along and be with him in his play. His mother demonstrates a capacity to "wait and see," a tolerance for her son's choice of
activity. She seems bemused, not alarmed by his resourcefulness and
curious to follow along as passive observer, ensuring his safety without
intruding. All these formal aspects revealed in the play situation are indications of a secure relationship between mother and child.

In the clinical presentation of Johnny as a "door slammer," engaged in
the repetitive activity of opening and closing doors, the formal aspects of
the play activity are vastly different. In this scenario Johnny is the solo
player. There is no interaction with others in his play. Rather, Johnny
initiates and maintains his play activity without regard to the actions of
others. His mother experiences this absorption in his own activity as
rejection, and she then becomes less available to her child. He remains
isolated in his play, an activity that continues to absorb his full attention.
Johnny seems to be playing entirely within the macrosphere, without
regard to the effects of his actions on the object, the door he is slamming.
The effects of his play resonate throughout the house, since they are not
contained within the safe microsphere of small objects. What is most
worrisome is that Johnny has little sense of the potential risk to himself or
others as a result of his activity.

The formal aspects of Johnny's play have clear implications for the
formation of a therapeutic alliance. Johnny is not used to playing with
others, and he feels no need to relate to others in his play. Johnny would not
perceive a need to change his behavior; to the contrary, he experiences a
need to persist in his behavior at all costs. An alliance with Johnny would
need to focus on gaining more understanding about the meaning of this
play activity, rather than immediately eliminating it from his repertoire of
play activities. It is impossible to consider a therapeutic alliance with
Johnny without considering the nature of the therapeutic alliance with his
parents. In fact, it is the dyad that seems to be in trouble here, a child who is
out of bounds and a mother who is experiencing increasing alienation from
him. The roles of the father and other siblings in the family, although
absent in the brief description of Johnny's problem, are also important.

Decentering Johnny from the role of the "problem child" is clearly an important therapeutic task. Johnny's play activity might best be understood within the larger context of family patterns of communication, broadening the foundation for a beginning understanding for therapeutic work.

Revisiting Jane

Jane sets the scene for her play activity in the presence of another. Although the other does not interact in any way, the presence of another person is an important frame of reference for Jane's play activity. Jane carefully arranges her toys before beginning to play. This pre-play activity indicates a preparation of structure within which the play activity will take place. It is more than just the "setting of a scene." Jane's pre-play activity is also an assignment of place for certain objects: a place for doll play, a place for listening to stories, a place for construction, a place for "show and tell." We comprehend Jane's understanding of sequencing and different types of play activity. Not everything happens at once; for each play activity there is a time and place. Jane seems to be the master of her miniature world. Although she plays alone, she is supported by the watchful presence of another and can evoke a variety of potential interactions for play. What activity does she choose to enact? Will she initiate interaction between her players?

Jane uses fantasy to play out the day in her imaginary school. She can enliven several characters, speaking for each one. This is an active, detailed microsphere that parallels Jane's own daily experience. Several children are playing house, taking the roles of different family members. While one child builds, another intrudes upon him aggressively and upsets his building. The teacher quells this disruption. Then, however, a mother brings her crying child to school, but the child does not want to stay and continues to cry. The crying becomes contagious with the other children and Jane interrupts her play activity. The protective boundary of the microsphere has been breached, and the play activity is ended. Jane goes to search for her mother, who is elsewhere in the house, as a point of reference.

The script for Jane's play activity is diverse and well articulated. It reflects her subjective experience of daily events, as well as her adaptive capacities in play. In Jane's case, these adaptive capacities for play clearly parallel her emotional development. She readily interacts with others and can function independently, but her autonomy can be compromised by moments of separation anxiety. Her relationships are secure and she is able to reference a caregiver to allay her anxiety. She is capable of referencing despite physical distance and can actively search for comfort. At these junctures, however, she must abandon her ongoing play activity. An alliance with Jane could easily be constructed around her capacity to play. She can initiate and facilitate play activity, used for fantasy play and for problem-solving. Jane feels secure and trusting in relationships with caregivers, a positive indication for her further development.

In the case of Jane as a clinic patient, the profile of play activity is very different. Instead of sustained play activity, there are short segments of play activity alternating with non-play activity. Each time Jane references her mother, she ends her play activity. The setting of the play activity remains within the microsphere, and the complex interactions between play characters reflect a developed level of social understanding. Each transition back into play activity requires a reorganization, however, and detracts from the overall flow of fantasy. Mother is unable to intervene effectively to allay her daughter's anxiety while she is playing. Instead, the locus of control remains solely with the child. When mother tries to intervene to be one of the characters, the child resists her participation.

The therapeutic alliance will be difficult to form with Jane, as she will probably perceive the therapist as a threatening stranger. It may be necessary for mother to remain in the room for some time before Jane feels sufficient comfort to be alone in the room with the therapist. Although Jane is spontaneous in beginning the play activity, she is inhibited in bringing the play to the level of satiation because of her anxiety. She is never completely absorbed in the play activity but is continuously surveying her surroundings to reference her mother. This play behavior suggests some conflict surrounding autonomous functioning and the resolution of tasks. Jane's strength is in her use of the microsphere and fantasy to organize her play activity.

Revisiting Tom

Tom is fully engrossed in his efforts to be successful in shooting baskets. He is playing alone, but it is easy to imagine his being involved with several other boys, shooting baskets together. Tom initiates and facilitates his play. There is no evidence of play inhibition. Tom's play is both gross motor play and fantasy play. Tom is not by himself; he is playing in view of a whole group of encouraging spectators. The ball play occurs within the macrosphere, assuring Tom's competence in the everyday world. His game has its own intrinsic motivation, yet Tom is able to respond to limits and ends his play in time for supper.

In the more problematic presentation of Tom, he initiates his play but is unable to facilitate or sustain it. His father seems to inhibit the play, as do his peers. Once the initial interest in playing diminishes, Tom ends the play by shifting to non-play. His isolated, negativistic stance leaves his parents troubled, and they are unable to talk as a family about the issues involved. What began as an exciting enterprise ends with disappointment and estrangement. The cessation of play seems indicative of avoidance of conflict that requires further exploration. The issues take place within the macrosphere, where Tom is unable to resolve his difficulties.

This chapter has considered the uniqueness and value of play activity for the developing child. Procedures were described for the segmentation of a child's activity in a therapy session, highlighting the category of play activity. Descriptive analysis of play activity segments was outlined, including the classification of types of play activity, the script (stage directions) for the play activity, and the spheres of play activity. Finally, these categories were used to analyze the play activity of three children whose play introduced the chapter.

Chapter 1 introduces structural analysis, a detailed enumeration of the separate processes that contribute to the formation of play activity. To illustrate these processes an entire therapeutic session of Ben, age three and one half years, is described. The play session is segmented, and then the descriptive categories outlined in the present chapter are used to get an overall perspective on the unfolding of Ben's play. Then, the new categories of affect, cognition, narrative, and developmental level are applied with an analysis of the structural components underlying Ben's play activity.

CHAPTER I

Structural Analysis of Play Activity

Unimpaired playfulness not only endows events categorized as play; it is so much a part of being active and alive that it soon tends to elude any definition except, perhaps, one that can include this elusive quality. (Erikson 1977, p.42)

The focus of this book is on play activity, specifically play activity in the therapy session: the forms it takes, its underlying structure, and the various functions it serves for the child. In the last chapter, play activity was described analytically and distinguished from other forms of the child's activity in the session. In this chapter, the structure of the play activity is analyzed into several components: *affective* components, *cognitive* components, *narrative* components, and *developmental* components. Chapters 3 to 6 then elaborate the functional analysis of play behavior, the *coping–defensive strategies* that can be seen in a child's play activity.

The affective, cognitive, narrative, and developmental components of the structure of play activity are separate aspects that work in unison. They can be considered dimensions of play activity to be measured individually, but they always act together to produce play activity. In later sections of this chapter, each of these components will be described in detail, with respect to both its theoretical relationship to the development of a child's play and its observation in the play activity. First, to illustrate how each of these components can be seen to contribute to the overall play activity, a summary of a session from the therapy of a three-and-a-half-year-old boy is given.

Ben's Therapy Session

The session described is the second session of Ben's therapy. He has been referred for consultation because of aggressive behavior at home and in daycare. His parents have recently divorced and share custody of their child. He comes to the session in the company of his nanny. The segmentation of the session is described below.

Segmentation of the Session

Session Segment One: Non-Play Activity #1

Ben lingers outside the door, clinging to his nanny's hand. The therapist goes out to greet him. Ben smiles a small smile and slowly follows her into the office. He instructs his nanny to wait for him in the waiting room.

Session Segment Two: Pre-Play Activity #1

Ben begins to examine plastic animal models he had been playing with in the previous session. He takes the animals out of the box and lines one up next to the other.

Ben: (To therapist) Do you remember these?

He grins and talks in a loud excited voice. He arranges the animals in family groupings. He labels them "mommy," "daddy," "sister," "brother," "baby."

Session Segment Three: Play Activity #1

Ben runs, grabs plastic knights and throws them to the ground. He recreates a fight scene from the previous session. Ben animates the soldiers with loud "fighting" noises. Ben forcefully smashes the figures into each other and then throws the animals onto the pile. He is breathing heavily and grimacing, making powerful movements with the figures as they smash into each other.

Suddenly, Ben jumps up and grabs a plastic hammer. He announces "the house is broken" and runs to the wall and bangs with the hammer. Given his high level of energy and affect, he is somewhat restrained in his hammering.

Therapist: Oh, dear...the house is broken!

Ben: *(Yelling, with fear, anxiety, and anger in his tone of voice)* Oh dear, the house is broken!

Ben is very agitated. Therapist moves closer to Ben.

Therapist: I bet the people in the house are upset!

Ben: Yes!

Ben rushes to the toy tool box and grabs a drill used in the last session as a gun. Ben jumps around the room in different positions, aiming the gun and yelling. Then he drops the gun and runs to the doll house.

Session Segment Four: Pre-Play Activity #2

Ben arranges the doll figures. He puts mommy, daddy, boy, and girl dolls in their own beds. Then he puts the baby doll in the daddy's bed. Ben describes his actions in a loud voice.

Session Segment Five: Play Activity #2

Suddenly, Ben grabs the doll figures and the furniture by the fistful and throws them out of the house into a heap on the floor. Ben backs away from the characters he is setting up and wanders around the room breathing heavily.

Therapist: *(Animating boy doll)* Oh, oh, we've fallen out of our house! Help! Help!

Ben tries to toss the father figure back into the house through the doll house window and then tosses him out again several times.

Ben: *(Yelling)* He's trying to fly into the house!

Therapist: Is daddy trying to get back home?

Ben drops the dolls, stomps on them, kicks the doll furniture and figures.

Session Segment Six: Non-Play Activity #2

Ben leaves the play space and wanders aimlessly around the room.

Session Segment Seven: Play Activity #3

Ben takes the bucket of Legos to the middle of the room. The therapist moves closer to him. Ben engages in five minutes of focused effort trying to construct a car he saw pictured on the bucket. Occasionally he asks the therapist to help put pieces together. He is much calmer, and the therapist admires his work.

Ben sees a propeller piece and turns the car into an airplane. He becomes frustrated as the pieces do not fit together. He pulls the dump truck over and piles it high with doll figures, furniture, and Lego pieces and then dumps them out. He does this several more times, becoming agitated and louder. Ben jumps up and goes to a table with paper, crayons, and pencils. He grabs a red pencil and begins stabbing the paper, yelling that it is a picture of all the shooting that is going on. Ben attacks the paper with the pencil, making slashes and jabs and yelling "Shoot! Shoot!"

Session Segment Eight: Interruption #1

Ben suddenly grabs the paper, says he is going to show it to his nanny, and runs out the door. The therapist follows and explains to the astonished woman that Ben wanted her to see his picture, as he pushes it in the nanny's face and runs back into the room. Ben is now very agitated and angry.

Session Segment Nine: Play Activity #4

Ben runs around the room. He jumps into different positions yelling "Shoot the Beast!" aiming first at the Lego construction, then at the wall, then at the door. After each yell, Ben races back to the table, grabs a different pencil, and makes slash marks and jabs at a piece of paper.

Ben:	*(To therapist)* Are you scared of the Beast?
Therapist:	*(Picks up boy doll)* That's a big, scary beast! Can someone help me?

Ben races over and knocks boy doll out of therapist's hand.

Ben:	*(Yelling)* Kill the Beast!

Ben grabs the toy drill and shoots at the boy doll. He lunges towards the couch, where he falls onto his stomach. He lies there quietly for a few moments as his breathing slows.

Therapist:	*(Goes to the chair next to the couch and sits for a few moments)* We have five minutes left in the session. Would you like to build more cars?
Ben:	*(Jumping up)* No.

Ben runs to retrieve a nerf ball, which he tries to toss into the basketball hoop. Most of his tosses are unsuccessful, but he is very proud of his successes. Therapist praises him. Ben opens the door with a few minutes remaining in the session.

Session Segment Ten: Non-Play Activity #3

Ben greets his nanny, and they prepare to leave. Good-byes are said. The therapist returns to office and hears Ben arguing with his nanny that he wants to stay. After a few minutes, she succeeds in coaxing him out into the hall. They leave the building together.

This session is a very revealing one. Although therapist and child patient have met only once before, the child has a lot to share and his therapist is ready to listen. The sequence of segments consists of play activity interspersed with pre-play and non-play. There are two pre-play segments, four play activity segments, and three non-play activity segments. An interruption reflects mounting tension within the child that cannot be contained within the session.

Ben usually initiates the play activity and ends the play activity segments. The therapist's main role is facilitative. One exception to this allocation of roles occurs in play activity segment #4, when the therapist animates the boy doll. Although Ben does briefly respond to her initiative, rather than rescuing the boy doll he shoots at him! This last play activity segment then shifts to throwing baskets and is ended by the therapist because the session is ending. Ben cannot depend upon her for closure and leaves a few minutes before the session is to end, only to complain to his nanny that he wants to stay longer.

Most of the play activity of this session takes place within the microsphere, as Ben plays with the doll house, animals, and family figures. When the small toy pieces cannot remain intact, he enters the macrosphere, using paper and pencil as props. Threatening fantasy play then invades his everyday world, and Ben seems mortally wounded as he takes refuge on the couch.

Therapist's Process Notes of the Therapy Session

The source for the description of Ben's therapeutic hour was the therapist's process notes of the entire therapeutic session. These process notes form a data base for segmentation and for deriving ratings of the structure of the child's play activity.[1] Capturing the content of a therapeutic hour is a challenge to all therapists. The therapist must include in the description of the therapeutic process the sequences of events, the child's behaviors and affects, the themes expressed, and specific dialogues. The therapist's detailed summary of a therapy session contains many levels of subjectivity. It conveys her experience of the session and her efforts to bring order and coherence to these events. The therapist's narrative of the therapeutic hour resonates with her own subjective experience as well as with ongoing inter-actions within the session. It is the therapist's perspective on how the child strives to bring meaning to his internal world.

Review of the process notes of Ben's therapeutic hour reveals a clear subplot to all the events occurring in the play activity. Ben communicates clearly his wish to be in charge. He walks into the room, sets the stage carefully for play, and begins to narrate the events of his story. He is unable to stay in control, however, as tensions escalate following his announcement that " The house is broken!" At this juncture, the content of the child's narrative punctures the continuity of the play activity. His upset cannot be

---

1   The reader is reminded most of the subscales use a 5-point Likert scale. In rating an attribute the key to each of these 5 points is as follows: 1 = no evidence; 2 = minimal evidence; 3 = moderate evidence; 4 = considerable evidence; 5 = most characteristic. Note: The affective component has its own unique descriptors. A few scales are rated on a 2-point scale; 0 = attribute absent; 1 = attribute present. (Kernberg, Chazan, & Normandin 1997).

contained, and the therapist is activated to bring him back to the business of playing. Again, tensions mount, this time around the daddy doll and his whereabouts. The play activity is broken off again. Ben tries to reinstate both his role as leader and his own equilibrium. He chooses to do a quiet construction play activity that brings him into partnership with the therapist. This balance is upset soon again, with Ben being overwhelmed by his own fears and anxieties. The appearance of the Beast causes an interruption to the session as Ben runs to his nanny for solace. He reenters, shoots at the little boy doll, and reasserts his role as initiator by choosing to aim at a basketball hoop. The therapist supports his successes but must caution Ben of the impending end of the session. Ben cannot bear to wait and hastens the end by adhering to his own self-imposed time limit. Upon separating from the therapist, however, Ben's conflict about separating is not resolved. He quickly laments having to leave, enacting his ambivalent feelings with his nanny.

In this instance, the interpersonal saga is reflected in Ben's story of destruction and mounting violence. The Beast cannot be contained and must be killed. The therapist must be kept passive or negated. The danger of aggression is very great, and these aggressive impulses threaten to destroy Ben's creative efforts at construction and ball play. The therapist's role as facilitator and protector cannot be maintained when these dangerous impulses are aroused. Ben flees his surroundings to escape the danger, but then he loses the companionship of his partner in play, the therapist.

Ben's struggle to play reflects his struggle in life. His play narrative is his attempt to assign meaning to the bits and pieces of his life that will not fit together. Coherence is lost when the house is "broken." Dad's flight through the air reveals Ben's anxieties concerning his father's whereabouts and his sense of desperation as he runs and stomps around the room. His agitated breathing, stomping movements, and loud voice clearly convey the urgency of the moment.

The therapist's narrative of Ben's activity provides a subjective envelope containing the drama and interaction of the session. It is the running record of what occurs and the meaning ascribed to these behaviors and events by the therapist. As was noted earlier, these process notes formed the basis for sorting Ben's activity during the session into segments of pre-play activity, play activity, non-play activity, and interruptions.

Often the longest play activity segment in a therapeutic session is the one selected for further structural analysis. In other instances, more than one play activity segment from the same therapeutic session is studied. In the case of three-and-a-half-year-old Ben, all the play activity segments are analyzed together to yield one global rating of the structure of his play activity. The rationale for doing a combined analysis is that no single play activity segment is representative of his general level of functioning. In Ben's case, analysis of the entire sequence of intermittent play activity segments renders a better assessment of his current play activity status.

Affective Components

Affect and the Development of Play

Affective components of the play activity are central to the communication of the child's subjective experience. Feelings expressed by the child are the earliest signals to the caregiver initiating interaction with him. Smiling and crying are the first signs of feelings conveyed by the infant. The parent responds to her child's signals, amplifying his feeling states. This early resonance between parent and child has been termed "primary intersubjectivity." Trevarthen (1980) has described the motivated search by the young infant for these target experiences contained in the expression of their mental states to others. These dyadic mirroring transactions trigger the attachment motivational system (Lichtenberg 1989), and the dyad enters into a "reciprocal reward system" (Emde 1989).

Findings from psychoanalysis, neuroscience, and infant research emphasize the role that positive feelings play in the organization of developmental progress (Emde 1992; Izard 1991; Lipsett 1976; Stern 1990). Attachment theory and object relations theory stress that it is pleasure and joy, rather than the diminution of tension, that are sought by the child and motivate his activities. Regulation of feeling states to optimal levels of stimulation occurs within the dyad, fostering development of the self and social ties. The caregiver acts as an auxiliary ego facilitating the infant's information processing by adjusting the mode, amount, and timing of information to the infant's integrative capacities (Papousek & Papousek 1987). An essential function of the parent is to permit the child to bear increasingly intense affective stimulation and then to step in and comfort the child before his feelings overwhelm him (Krystal 1978).

As the child grows, he communicates with his caregiver using distal-visual receptors, rather than proximal-tactile receptors. He is able to "social reference" his parent from a greater distance, process information more rapidly, and return for refueling (Mahler, Pine, & Bergman 1975) when necessary. These refueling activities represent highly condensed symbiotic merger experiences that enrich the physical environment and expand the orbit of play activity (Rose 1972). Later, as the child expands his world of play and encounters expected disorganization and displeasure, it is the reattunement of the attachment bond that enables the child to repair and develop a sense of himself as effective.

Reattunement takes place in the arena of play activity where the child reengages with that part of his world that is joyful and reliable. This is the parental function referred to by Winnicott (1971, p.10) as "good-enough holding." What the child internalizes is the relationship—his role and aspects of the caregiver's role in the caregiving relationship. In play activity these relationships can be observed "in situ." It is not only the other actual person with whom the child interacts; by the second year the child develops symbolic dynamic interactive representations. The child then interacts with a symbolic as well as an actual other (Greenberg & Mitchell 1983). Negative emotions, including shame, protest, aggression, humiliation, and rage, emerge when the caregiver is unable to facilitate an optimum resolution of very high levels of emotional arousal. These negative emotions when uncontained can lead to interruptions in play activity, disorganization of affect state, and failure of coping responses.

In sum, affective development is the source and continuing essence of play activity. The child's feelings are heavily contingent upon his relationships to his caregivers. These attachment bonds extend the safe arena of play and the child's repertoire of play activities. Play interruptions are experienced when affective regulation is impaired and cannot be reinstated. The optimum balance in affective regulation is sought by both caregiver and child, to enable the expansion of the joyful, enhancing arena of play.

Affective Components Observed in Play Activity

Table 1.1 Affective Components Observed in Play Activity

1. **Overall Hedonic Tone**
   - Obvious Pleasure
   - Pleasurable Interest
   - Natural Interest
   - Sober
   - Overt Distress

2. **Spectrum of Affects**
   - Very Wide
   - Wide
   - Medium
   - Narrow
   - Constricted

3. **Regulation and Modulation of Affects**
   - Very Flexible
   - Somewhat Flexible
   - Medium
   - Somewhat Rigid
   - Very Rigid

4. **Transitions between Affective States**
   - Always Abrupt
   - Usually Abrupt
   - Fluctuates
   - Usually Smooth
   - Always Smooth

5. **Appropriateness of Affect to Content**
   - Always
   - Usually
   - Sometimes
   - Rarely
   - Never

6. **Child's Affective Tone towards Therapist**
   - Very Positive
   - Somewhat Positive
   - Neutral
   - Somewhat Negative
   - Very Negative

7. **Therapist's Affective Tone towards Child**
   - Very Positive
   - Somewhat Positive
   - Neutral
   - Somewhat Negative
   - Very Negative

Table 1.1 outlines the affective components of the child's play activity that can be observed in the therapy session. The therapist first assesses the child's *overall hedonic tone,* the sum of the types and range of emotions in a child's play. Play that is satisfying and fulfilling is experienced by the child as pleasurable and affords him the opportunity to express a variety of affects. At the other extreme, overt distress, like fear or crying, may result in play ending in disruption or lead to a segment of interruption.

In our clinical example of three-and-a-half-year-old Ben, the overall hedonic tone is one of overt distress. Ben cannot sustain pleasurable feelings, as the house is "broken." He creates chaos, throwing the toys around the room. His efforts to restore affective equilibrium are ineffective. Even when resorting to more neutral toys (Legos) he is unable to attain an affective balance and repeatedly becomes agitated and distressed. Only by "killing the Beast" can he feel mastery and enjoy shooting baskets. There is considerable evidence for a wide *spectrum of affects* as he swings from pleasure to fear and overwhelming anxiety. His *regulation and modulation* of feelings is moderately rigid as he attempts to cope with the mounting intensity of his feelings. He knocks the boy doll out of the therapist's hand and grabs the toy drill to shoot the boy doll. It is only then that he is able to gradually recover. There is considerable evidence of abrupt *transitions* between affective states as the feelings appear to be almost leaping out of his control. In the play activity Ben expresses feelings of excitement, aggression, anger, anxiety, fear, and finally pleasure, feelings that are characteristically *appropriate* to the content of his play. Ben is usually positive in his feelings for his therapist; similarly, the feelings the therapist expresses towards Ben are usually positive.

Cognitive Components
Cognitive Components and the Development of Play

Early consistent perceptual-action patterns and consistency of affective experience give coherence to the infant's emerging sense of core self (Beebe & Stern 1977; Lichtenberg 1989; Stern 1985). The infant ties together his experiences through the use of perceptual memory. Louis Sander (1975) introduced the concept that otherness and self-regulation are always interconnected. Thus, the quality and experience of care received in earliest relationships becomes inextricably bound up with the child's experience of himself. As the child grows, his social interactions multiply and become more complex. These experiences with his surroundings are stored in memory and assume an independent status as representations. The child represents animate persons, living creatures, and plants differently from inanimate objects. Sandler and Rosenblatt (1962) referred to this emergent subjective surround as the representational world of the child.

Piaget (1954) termed this differential in the development of cognitive representations "horizontal decalage"; in the usual course of development, a sense of permanence is constructed around persons earlier than around things. In research involving the child's search for the hidden object (hide and go seek), the appearance of this sequence of decalage depended upon the sensitivity of the mother, demonstrating the close attunement between the development of attachment and cognitive systems (Chazan 1981). The most contingent, attuned stimulus was the one that took dominance and developed earlier. Selma Fraiberg (1969) described the emergence of emotional, or libidinal, object constancy several months subsequent to object constancy. Libidinal object constancy implies constancy in emotional bond despite variation in experience. Thus, the child is able to conserve a positive emotional bond across diverse situations, because the symbolic representation of the caregiver remains stable, allowing for the formation of basic trust (Erikson 1950).

These cognitive and cognitive-affective structures bring about the child's enhanced sense of competence and self-efficacy. Lichtenberg (1989) described an exploratory–assertive system accounting for the child's motivation to problem-solve. When neither physiological nor attachment needs took precedence, the child found himself a niche of "open space" (Sander 1983) where exploration became actualized. At these moments, the infant could experience a relative disengagement from the caregiver and entertain himself. D. W. Winnicott (1958) called this state "the capacity to be alone in the presence of the other." In this space, the child discovers his own initiative and personal life, rather than remaining confined to a life reactive to external stimuli.

Play activity develops within this "open space," promoting assertiveness and independence. Early childhood games reflect the child's initiative at finding the lost, or hidden, object. Thus, Freud (1920) observed his grandson (who we are told was very attached to his mother) at age one and a half years invent a game of throwing away and searching for small objects. The infant expressed his interest and satisfaction by vocalizing a loud, long-drawn-out "oo-oo." A child's play during these moments retains the sense of still being in the presence of the caregiver. The child at play is contained by a "holding environment" (Winnnicott 1958). This metaphor suggests the child is playing within an extension of the caregiver's lap, a "background of safety" (Sandler 1960). Efficacy pleasure (White 1959; Lichtenberg 1989) occurs as the child experiences increasing levels of competence and branches out to explore further novel social and physical aspects of his environment. New cognitive activities are accompanied by a variety of contemplative affects and feelings of pleasure in mastery.

When solving a problem or telling a story, a child may invent private symbols—designating a table as a house, for instance—or use an object in a consensual way, such as using a small cup for setting a table for tea. The child himself determines the use of objects in the play activity, assigning meaning to evoke given affects. With this freedom the child can reinvent the problem and express his own personal way of pursuing possible solutions. With the introduction of symbolic thought (at about eighteen months of age), the universe becomes truly infinite, as the child strives to extend and reinvent the pleasure of assertion and exploration by himself and with others (Lichtenberg 1989).

Cognitive Components Observed in Play Activity

Table 1.2 Cognitive Components Observed in Play Activity

1. **Role Representation**
   - Complex – Dyadic
   - Solitary
   - Precursor
2. **Stability of Representation (Persons and Objects)**
   - Fluid/Stable
   - Voluntary/Involuntary
3. **Use of the Play Object**
   - Realistic
   - Substitution
   - Miming
   - Source of Activity
4. **Style of Representation (Persons and Objects)**
   - Realistic
   - Fantasy
   - Bizarre

Cognitive components of the play activity include the types of representations, or mental images, of persons and objects used by the child while playing, the use of these representations, and their style of representation (see Table 1.2). Each of these cognitive components will be considered separately.

While the child is playing he may choose to take on a role, or to be a certain character. *Role representation* can occur at different levels of elaboration: *complex, dyadic, solitary,* and *precursor* (Bretherton 1984).

Complex role-play is the highest level of role-play. It can take one of three forms: *collaborative* play, *directorial* play, or *narrator* play.

In collaborative play the child interacts with another person or uses dolls or miniature figures to enact several different roles. The child may utilize a variety of family roles (mother, father, baby), occupational roles (doctor, teacher, farmer), or fictional roles to tell his story. While playing the child coordinates his perspective with that of his co-player or co-players, who may be toys animated by the parent or therapist as well as by the child (Dunn & Dale 1984; Bretherton 1984).

In directorial play the child himself does not engage in the play activity but directs the play action, directing the other person, dolls, or miniature toys how to talk or act. The child is in charge of all the aspects of the play.

In narrator play the child becomes the narrator of his play, commenting on play events.

Dyadic role-play involves the representation of two roles. The child plays at being an active partner to another person or activated doll or toy.

Solitary role-play occurs when the child completely transforms himself into being someone else or activates a toy or doll and talks for the character (Piaget 1962).

Precursors to role-play are snatches or fragments, bits of a role that are not yet consolidated into a cohesive identity. There are four forms of precursors to role-play:

1. A child represents or imitates an aspect of his own behavior, indicating by gesture or intonation that he is pretending (Piaget 1962).

2. A child represents or imitates an aspect of another's behavior, indicating by gesture or intonation that he is pretending (Piaget 1962).

3. A child relates to others (persons, objects, toy animals) in his pretend play as if they were extensions of his own ideas,

without independent or reciprocal input. The other pretend person is not viewed as a partner; the child is not playing he is a different person but portraying what is done to himself (Piaget 1962; Nicholich 1977).

Fein and Apfel (1979) found that at 12 months 80 percent of the infants in their sample engaged in self-directed pretend feeding, 32 percent fed the mother or the experimenter, and only 19 percent fed a doll (forms of pretending were not mutually exclusive, so they add up to more than 100 percent). Further, since infants use a person as recipient of a symbolic scheme before they use a doll in the same fashion, there are grounds for assuming that the infant is using the doll as a human figure when doll-directed play does emerge. Inge Bretherton (1984) agreed with Greta Fein (1978, 1987) that gradually behaviors directed toward persons take a slightly different form from behaviors directed towards dolls. For example, infants expect adults and peers to cooperate when sipping tea from toy cups.

4.   The child plays in a parallel fashion with another doll or person. The child and the other are engaged in the same or similar activity without interacting with each other (Nicholich 1977).

When Ben begins his play with the toy animals he lines them up and assigns each a family role: "mommy, daddy, baby." These are followed by the animation of multiple knights and soldiers in battle. Both of these play segments characteristically contain examples of complex role-play, including narrator play and collaborative role-play.

Ben then animates each of the family members, placing them in their positions in the house and acting as narrator of what is happening. Later, after the therapist facilitates the play by activating the boy figure, Ben activates the father doll, who tries to "fly" back into the house. These play activities are considerable evidence of complex role-play.

Ben abandons his characters to engage in construction with Lego blocks. Following outbursts of aggression, Ben creates a new character, "the Beast." The encounter with this scary character is brief. The therapist facilitates dyadic role-play by again speaking for the boy doll: "That's a big, scary beast! Can anybody help me?" Ben responds by grabbing the toy drill and shooting at the boy doll. This confabulation of victim/attacker is confusing. Ben identifies the boy doll as the source of his terror and the target to be killed. Both the dangerous impulses and the need for rescue have been products of Ben's imagination, enacted in the form of dyadic roles. In the first instance, Ben is the little boy terrified by the Beast. Then a role reversal occurs; when the little boy doll calls out for help (in the voice of the therapist), Ben attacks him as the dangerous Beast. These play activities are all considerable evidence of dyadic role-play. In this session there are no examples of solitary role-play or precursors to role-play.

The representations of persons or toys depicted by the child may or may not undergo *transformation*. In the case of *voluntary* transformation the changes that occur in character or theme occur under the creative control of the child. These changes may be *fluid*, where several changes take place, or *stable*, where only one change takes place, as occurs in role reversal. *Involuntary* transformation occurs when the variation in play themes or roles occurs outside the child's control. He begins playing one theme or role and appears surprised, shocked, or frightened by the change.

In the case of Ben, representations in the play gradually progress from stable with no transformations to stable voluntary transformation to involuntary transformation. There is moderate evidence for each category. At first Ben aligns his toy animals and family dolls; these dolls retain their stable representation. The battling soldiers and knights also remain stable characters. The doll house remains a house but is damaged. The Lego car undergoes a transformation to a plane, under Ben's voluntary control. Suddenly, in a frightening way, the boy doll becomes a destructive Beast and must be killed. This menacing character, boy transformed to Beast, reflects Ben's mounting conflict surrounding discharge of his own frightening aggressive feelings.

The play objects (toys) may be used *realistically*, where a toy replica is used as it is used in real life. Alternatively, in symbolic play, *substitution* may occur. One play object is substituted for another, severing the meaning of the object from the real object. In some instances, the play objects are created through gesture, or *mime*. In more primitive play activity, the toy may be used only for its *sensory* qualities (Tustin 1990, 1972).

In Ben's play, there is considerable evidence of objects being represented realistically and minimal evidence of the substitution of one object for another. Ben used a pencil to represent a gun and shoot. In the case of

the "Beast," the boy doll became larger than life and was used to symbolically represent a scary creature.

Finally, the representations of persons and objects can be *realistic, magical*
(*fantasy*), or *bizarre*. In Ben's case, the characters and objects are most characteristically represented as having realistic attributes; for instance, a car is a
car, a house is a house. The father can fly through the air, however, and the
beast is menacing and terrifying, with inhuman qualities. Similarly, Ben
himself assumes superhuman strength to kill the beast. In these instances
there is moderate evidence of attributes of representations that are fantastic
or magical. There is no evidence of bizarre attributes in the characters or
objects portrayed.

Narrative Components
Narrative Components and the Development of Play

The cognitive and affective configurations of a child's play activity come
together in telling a story. The story to be told involves events and concerns
significant to the child. Sometimes the story unfolds in interaction as a
social game between therapist and child. At other times, the story is told
symbolically through characters invented for the purpose of communicating the child's imaginary experience. At still other times, telling the story
involves constructing and/or manipulating agreed-upon rules. In each case,
the story sequences events across time. Thus, the story of the play activity is
a framework for integrating disparate events that become organized, with a
beginning, a middle, and an end. This organization of the narrative of the
play activity is an integrative act containing the imprint of both child and
therapist.

Even as a passive participant the therapist contributes toward the formulation of a narrative. Minimally, she provides a context of a background of
safety. As has been noted, in other instances the therapist may become more
active as initiator or co-author. The role of the therapist is determined by the
child's level of competence and personal needs. Most importantly, it is to
support and facilitate the child's capacity to play. The therapist then elabo-
rates the play activity and encourages the development of the child's play
narrative.

Jerome Bruner (1990) has noted the importance of stories in helping a child to organize his experience. He traces the young child's sensitivity to human interaction in acts of giving and receiving and actions towards goals and their achievement. Thus, young children are profoundly aware of the "unexpected' in phrases such as "all gone' for completion and "uh oh' for incompletion. The earliest requirement of narrative is a focus on people and their actions, which dominate the child's interest and attention. The second requirement is the concentration of attention and information processing on the unusual; children most often gesture toward, vocalize at, and finally talk about what is different. The third requirement of narrative is the sequencing of subject-verb-object ("somebody does something'). Sequences are bound by the use of temporals ("then,' "later') and eventually by the use of causals. The fourth requirement of narrative is "voice' or perspective, which can be detected early in a child's development as varied vocal intonations (Stern 1977).

Jerome Bruner (1990) contended that the four prerequisites for narrative precede logical, rational thought and account for the child's early interest in and understanding of stories. Culture intervenes later to elaborate these protonarratives to include traditional ways of telling and interpreting. Bruner cites the example of Emily, whose narratives were recorded between ages 18 months and three years (Nelson 1989). In her autobiographical narratives about what she has been doing or what she anticipates doing the next day, Bruner discerns a constitutive function. Emily is not simply reporting; she is trying to make sense of her everyday life. "She seemed to be in search of an integral structure that could encompass what she had done with what she felt with what she believed' (p.89). To Bruner's ears, Emily's leaps forward in speech were spurred by a need to construct meaning, narrative meaning.

Involved in a similar endeavor, the therapist functions as the child's collaborator in working toward the formation of narrative meaning expressed in his play activity. The therapist facilitates narrative development by drawing attention to significant play happenings, elaborating the details of characters or events, ordering happenings into sequence by making associations between events, clarifying confusions or conflicts, and giving voice to the child's perspective. Finally, when appropriate, the therapist offers interpretations of the meaning of events of which the child may be unaware.

Through the medium of shared narrative the child gains an awareness not only of himself but also of the shared dimensions of human behavior (Engel 1999). Children as early as two years of age adopt formats such as games and conversations in order to share meanings and plans with others (Garvey 1977). Between the ages of three and four years, children's accounts of familiar events presume that their listeners share the same basic scripts for human routines (Schank & Abelson 1977). Understanding human behavior involves a sensitivity not only to how one is a separate being, but also to how one is similar to others.

Dennis Wolf, Jayne Rayne, and Jennifer Altshuler (1984) have presented data emphasizing the importance of symbolic play between the ages of two and three years for the development of social understanding. Using gesture and language the child is able to make explicit in play activity his understanding of how people think, feel, and act. Gender differences appear as early as four years in giving prominence to a sense of agency versus experience in understanding others. Girls were observed to emphasize what characters experience, while boys focused on what characters did and said. Thus, gender interacts with social knowledge (scripts) to produce different styles of social perception. The therapist works within different play styles to enhance the adaptation of her child patient.

The capacity for make-believe, a cognitive achievement, and the capacity to make meaning through storytelling derive from parent and child playing together, inventing games involving role-playing, with reference to nonpresent events, and focusing on unexpected outcomes (surprise). Likewise, peers, siblings, and therapist interact with the child in scripts that are expected and then revised in accordance with the story that unfolds.

NARRATIVE COMPONENTS OBSERVED IN PLAY ACTIVITY

Table 1.3 Narrative Components Observed in Play Activity

1. **Topic of the Play Activity**

2. **Theme of the Play Activity**

3. **Level of Relationship Portrayed within the Narrative**
    - Self
    - Dyadic
    - Triadic
    - Oedipal

4. **Quality of Relationship Portrayed within the Narrative**
    - Autonomous
    - Parallel
    - Dependent
    - Turning
    - Malevolent
    - Destructive
    - Annihilating

5. **Use of Language by the Child/by the Therapist**
    - Silence
    - Imitation
    - Pun/Rhyme
    - Single Role
    - Multiple Roles
    - Metaphor
    - Meaning
    - Something Other
    - Describing

Table 1.3 summarizes the narrative components that the therapist observes in the play activity. The *topic* of the play activity is chosen by the child to convey the content used in the construction of his story. The *theme* of the play activity involves the dynamics of the relationships and activities integral to the unfolding of the story. At times topic and theme can become enmeshed and are difficult to untangle. The story unfolding through the child's play activity has its own unique dynamics. Examining the types of relationships portrayed by the child in the play narrative reveals the relationships that interest him and that are animated by his imagination and curiosity.

The relationship portrayed within the play narrative may depict a single character, reflecting preoccupation with the *self*. When two characters are depicted, the *dyadic* level may involve themes of sameness/ differentness, coercion/submission, nurturance/dependency, or being paired. At the *triadic* level of relationship, interactions occur between several characters, each of which relates to the others in some way. On the *oedipal* level, the triadic relationships involve awareness of differences in generation, gender differences, or the exclusion of a third party from a mutual relationship.

Ben's play includes two generations, child and parents. He is clearly aware of gender differences, with greater focus on the father doll, the boy doll, and the villain beast, who is also clearly masculine. Although the female doll and children are background figures, the female therapist excluded from the main action is turned to at times for assistance. There is considerable evidence for dyadic level relationships in Ben's play activity and minimal evidence of triadic and oedipal relationships.

The *quality of relationship* portrayed within the play narrative can vary along a continuum from mutuality to destructiveness. Relationships depicted may be *autonomous* (independent relationships), *parallel* (relationships are similar and concurrent), *dependent* (one partner is dependent, or leaning, on the other partner), or *twinning* (both partners in the relationship are identical). Alternatively, they may reveal dynamics of *malevolent control* (one partner attempts to control the other partner with cruelty), *destruction* (an identifiable person, or force, destroys the other), or *annihilation* (complete destruction by an unidentifiable enveloping force) (Urist 1977).

Ben's play reveals considerable evidence of fear of malevolent control and moderate evidence of destruction and annihilation. The source of the danger is muddled; at times it seems to emerge from external sources, and at other times from Ben himself. This confusion is expressed in Ben's selection of the boy doll both to represent the Beast and to be attacked. Ben has experienced his own anger and aggressive impulses as threatening as the external danger, and the danger from within must then be destroyed via an external toy object.

The child's use of *language* to explicate his play can range from no communication to imitation of sounds to word play—puns and rhymes—and verbalization of a single or multiple roles. Talking during the play may occur within a metaphor or in indirect reference to the meaning of the play. The talk may describe the play or concern something other than the play. The therapist's use of language may be described using these same categories.

Ben combines narrative elements (topic, theme, language, relationships) to tell his story. A segment by segment analysis of the narrative components gives a sense of how the story unfolds.

In Play Activity Segment #1, the topic is war and battle; the theme is destruction. Ben depicts a battle scene between warring knights (dyadic) and then proceeds to "break" the house with all the family members in it (triadic) and ends by shooting a gun around the room. The relationships depicted in this narrative are destructive. Language is used by both Ben and therapist to describe the play events.

In Play Activity Segment #2, the topic is family life; themes include rescue, dispersal, falling, and separation. Ben depicts relationships between father and other family members, clearly aware of generational differences (oedipal). The play is characterized by an overpowering, enveloping force causing the children to fall and the father to fly through the air. All are being tossed about by a force completely out of their control. As Ben drops the figures and stomps on them, the play segment ends with annihilation. Ben uses language to describe the play; the therapist speaks for the characters, speaking within the play metaphor.

In Play Activity Segment #3, topics include construction and destruction; themes include building, collecting, dumping, shooting, and injury. There is no cohesive depiction of relationships between characters. Ben begins by building with Lego blocks and he asks the therapist to help him with his building. There is an ominous suggestion of destruction to come in

Ben's yelling and mounting aggressive attacks as his sense of frustration escalates when the pieces do not fit together.

In Play Activity Segment #4, topics include self-defense and ball playing; themes include killing and mastery. A destructive struggle breaks out between the Beast/Boy and Ben (dyadic) that ends in the destruction and death of the villain, while Ben plays at shooting baskets. Ben uses language to inquire about the meaning of the play for the therapist, asking: "Are you scared of the Beast?" Both therapist and Ben also use language to speak within the play metaphor.

Developmental Components

Table 1.4 Developmental Components Observed in Play Activity

1. **Chronological Developmental Level of Play Activity**
   - Very Immature
   - Somewhat Immature
   - Age Appropriate
   - Somewhat Advanced
   - Very Advanced

2. **Gender Identity of the Play Activity**
   - Predom Male
   - Predom Female
   - No Predom

3. **Social Level of the Play Activity (Interaction with Therapist)**
   - Isolated/Unaware
   - Isolated/Aware
   - Parallel
   - Reciprocal
   - Cooperative

---

4. **Psychosexual Level**
   - Oral
   - Anal
   - Phallic
   - Oedipal
   - Latency

5. **Separation – Individuation Level**
   - Differentiation
   - Practicing
   - Rapprochement
   - Constancy

Developmental Components Observed in Play Activity

A developmental trajectory implies the successive unfolding of stages of play, one stage following the other in a sequential manner, arranged hierarchically with each level building on the prior level and extending beyond it. From a developmental perspective, play activity is seen to follow a path of increasing complexity depending on chronological age, social level, psychosexual stage, and level of individuation. Table 1.4 lists these developmental components. Gender of the child is a pervasive influence on the development of play activity. Gender identity interacts with all of the above-mentioned developmental components to influence patterns of play activity (Youngblade & Dunn 1995). Because of its multidimensional influence on development, gender identity is listed as a developmental component of play.

EXPECTED CHRONOLOGICAL LEVELS OF PLAY ACTIVITY

An important criterion in assessing a child's development is whether or not he can play at a level expected for his chronological age. According to Anna Freud (1965), one indication of an emotional problem is a child's wish to be younger than his chronological age. Alternatively, a precocious child may pursue interests appropriate for an older child. Often, a child shows variability in his play interests, having some interests at age level and others at variance with age expectations. Some variability in interests is expected;

it is only when a child completely diverges from his age-expected play activities that there is cause for concern.

Following is a brief outline of the expected chronological progression in play activity from birth to age nine years (Greenspan 1991; Garner 1998; Johnson 1998).

Birth to Twelve Months

The child's activity centers about reciprocal interactions (for example, reaching out, pointing, dropping object) that become increasingly playful. Themes of simple games include recognition and reunion (such as peek-a-boo). The child increasingly seeks out new activities to explore and to have fun. The child gradually becomes more interested in persons and things than his own body.

Appropriate materials at this age include toys encouraging reaching, grasping, seeing, and vocalizing, such as, mobiles, mirrors, bells, bubbles, water play, balls, rattles, beads, music box.

One to Two Years

The child continues to take delight in his own body movements, such as walking, climbing, pouring, joining parts of an object and taking them apart. He expresses his needs via pointing and naming objects, and taking mother to the shelf to get a toy. Increased initiative is demonstrated in prolonged sequences of activity; for example, a doll is hugged, spanked, and then hugged again. The child enjoys games of peek-a-boo and patty cake as well as simple songs and mirroring games involving copying sounds and gestures. Dramatic role-playing begins as the child plays at mothering mother (turning passive into active) and at performing mother's activities. Memory is used to recall where objects have been hidden in several places. The mirror is used to reflect the child's image pleasurably from different perspectives.

Play materials at this age include pull toys, hammer toys, dolls, blocks, doll house (small), large crayons, and sand and water play. The child enjoys listening to music and stories, turning the thick pages of a picture book, and playing with a special cherished furry animal.

Two to Three Years

The child's play becomes more symbolic and interactive. The child can play at being an imaginary creature, imitate an adult role, and project his wishes onto another. Much of the play centers upon what the child has seen or heard in his real-life experience. Dramatic play continues to develop in the context of dyadic relationships, as in the leaving game and the hiding game. Cross-identification in dyadic play ("you be me and I'll be you") indicates an increased capacity to understand others on the basis of similarity.

Favored materials are dolls, stuffed animals, materials for messes (sponges, small containers, bubbles), clay, crayons for drawing strokes and circles, small objects for sorting into categories based on color, shape, and size.

Three to Six Years

Themes of play are extended and elaborated with the further development of language. Specifically, multiple characters appear and are coordinated around a story. The child shows interest in themes of power, superheroes, space and rocket ships, monsters, witches, and other characters from fairy tales and comics, although he realizes that his play is "just make-believe." Dyadic issues include having a special friend, overcoming a more powerful figure, and being cared for exclusively. Stories are told with an interest in new words and exaggeration and in how things happen. Gender differentiation in preferences for toys and play themes begins to emerge. Miniature worlds become the focus for play, including toy soldiers and small construction toys. Props and costumes are important for pretend play. At this age children enjoy making potions and endowing them with magical powers as an antidote to their fears. These fears include bodily injury, thunder, wind, fire, wild animals, darkness, loss of love. Alphabet and number facts form the basis for new games. Simple board games are played, but the child needs to win and does not understand that rules are for everyone. He often makes up rules of his own, disrupts a game in order to reverse positions, and is intolerant of defeat. Fine motor tasks include coloring, collages, clay, and jigsaw puzzles.

Appropriate play materials for this age group include props and costumes for dramatic play, blackboard, dolls, superheroes, miniature figures, small animals and vehicles, clay, paints, crayons, pasting materials, and scissors. Simple board games and card games (such as *Candyland, Chutes and Ladders, Junior Uno, Junior Monopoly,* and *Junior Clue*). Other objects that may interest the child are a calendar, a clock, a telephone, a magnifying glass, an indoor basketball hoop, musical instruments, rhythm band instruments, trucks, wagons, cars, and trains.

Seven to Nine Years

Entrance into latency is accompanied by a sharp diminution in pretend play, which becomes more covert in the form of daydreaming. The child plays at many different roles and narrates long and varied stories, describing many-faceted characters. He can play at who he will become (parent, sports hero, president), or at being a member of the opposite gender, or at breaking rules. Although the child knows that rules exist and wants to respect them, he sometimes insists on interpreting rules as he understands them. Fairness is an important issue. In board games, when faced with defeat the child may give excuses or claim that he was cheated or that the play was unfair. Gender differentiation is also obvious, with boys tending toward active and competitive sports and girls preferring less competitive and more group-oriented activities, such as jump rope, jacks, and skating. The child develops a clear sense of the difference between reality and fantasy and knows different rules apply. Collections of objects expand, reflecting the child's interests. Interest in magic tricks develops, and the child likes to "be in the know." Jokes and caricatures including familiar and famous people are enjoyed. Stories are often accompanied by drawings, depicting fantasy or battle scenes. Children begin to play musical instruments and to take part in plays, acrobatics, swimming, and ballet.

Materials used in play include an expanded array of board games (such as, *Monopoly, Clue,* dominoes, pick-up-sticks, knock hockey, chess, checkers, chinese checkers, *Othello*) and card games. Children collect various objects, often to use in trading. Art supplies include paints, clay, drawing and collage materials. Props are used for dramatic presentations, usually with prepared script. Some popular toys are indoor basketball hoops, jump ropes, balls, jacks, marbles, manipulatives to measure volume and temperature, a globe, magnet sets, science kits and simple carpentry tools.

The child's play activity is evaluated in relation to the *expected chronological level* and *gender identity*. In a schematic assessment of developmental level, Ben's play activity is clearly a bit advanced for his chronological age (three and one half years), approximating the play of a child between three and six years of age. He is able to compose a narrative consisting of several interacting roles (family members) and compose a miniature world (the house). His play theme contains a fear of disaster (broken and falling persons and things) and an attempt to defend himself against these threatening events. These fears are expected at three and a half years, but they are intensified by Ben's chaotic family situation. Ben's Lego construction is both adept and calming. As the character of the Beast emerges, with all its menacing attributes and self-reference, we have the first sense of deterioration of differentiation between reality and fantasy; in his earlier play, Ben seemed to have this distinction clearly in place. Finally, Ben's interest in the basketball hoop and competence in shooting baskets suggest the play of an older child. The aggressive themes and activity within the narrative are also consonant with masculine interests.

Selman (1980) outlines five levels in the development of a child's *social interaction*. The levels form a developmental hierarchy. On the first level (*isolated play-unaware*) the child is playing by himself and unaware of his isolation; he may or may not be in the presence of another person. On level two (*playing alone*) the child is aware he is playing alone. On level three (*parallel play*) children play at similar activities alongside each other without interacting. On level four (*reciprocal play*) there is give and take between the players. At the highest level (*cooperative play*) mutual cooperation occurs with joined efforts to reach a common goal.

Ben plays reciprocally with his therapist most of the time. There is give and take between them as he sets up the family house, builds his Legos (therapist helps Ben to put the pieces together), and tries to cope with the Beast (Ben and therapist fight the Beast together). Even the solitary activity of basketball is marked by appreciation the therapist expresses. The therapist's participation is crucial to Ben, and he relies upon her facilitation of the play to keep it ongoing.

The child's play activity can also be analyzed from the perspective of *psychosexual stage* (Peller 1954; Tyson & Tyson 1990). *Oral* components of the play activity include the "taking in" of external stimulation through the various senses (visual, auditory, kinesthetic). The child may be the recipient or the donor of the nurturing activities.

Anal components of the play activity focus around the themes of "retaining" or "letting go." The former may be associated with badness, while the latter may be associated with something valued, treasured, or good; the reverse can also be true. The main focus of the child in these activities is control and regulation. Play activities such as splashing, messing, and gluing derive from the basic body functions of urinary and bowel control, revealing both the desire to soil and make a mess and then the reaction against that desire, the striving to clean and organize.

Phallic components of the play activity are characterized by penetration and thrust into the environment or other person. They are usually represented by gun play or by entering into an enclosure. This type of play activity may contain elements of exhibitionism. The child likes to show off how big he is, how strong he is, or parts of his body.

Oedipal components of play activity have the following three aspects: at least three characters are involved; two of the characters are a pair, with an excluded third party who is of a different generation; and an awareness of differences between the sexes is expressed or implied. Oedipal themes include issues of competition, rivalry, and exclusion. Characteristic oedipal feelings include success, jealousy, and envy.

Latency components of play activity are focused on issues of morality and fairness. Sublimating earlier psychosexual issues, the latency child focuses on compliance with rules and imitation of societal roles. Latency play activities are concerned with performing adult tasks such as construction, drawing, and imitating occupational pursuits. Magic tricks, in which the child using magical powers reverses roles, thereby bewildering the adult, are also a latency activity (Sarnoff 1976).

Ben's play activities are primarily focused around the threat of aggression and destruction. These play activities are phallic and intense in their thrusting, powerful stance—the soldiers battle each other, smashing into each other; Ben bangs the house with a hammer and rushes around the room aiming a gun. There is some conflict over the hammering; the therapist notes that Ben is somewhat restrained in his hammering, given his high degree of energy. The construction activity with Legos is latency play, counterbalancing the more battling stance of the previous play themes.

Phallic activities return, with the stabbing of the paper with a red pencil and the shouts of "Shoot, shoot." These impulses threaten to disorganize Ben, and he leaves the room to the security of his nanny. He returns to the play activity, once again grabbing the drill and shooting before falling onto his stomach and breathing slowly. Basketball, latency-phase play activity, restores his equilibrium.

In sum, there is some evidence of anal concerns, as Ben seems to explode and "let go" of the tension inside him. The dominant components of the play activity, however, are phallic, aggressive, attacking, expressions of penetration, dominance and submission. Reparative, restorative feelings are expressed through latency play activities. These variable levels of psychosexual development generally reflect play activity that is advanced for Ben's chronological age.

Issues of *separation—individuation* refer to the child's resolution of his conflicts surrounding being autonomous from his parent and attaining his own individual unique characteristics. The levels in this process of development include: *differentiation*—issues of being the same or being different (for example, the child contrasts big from little, me from you, black skin from white skin); *practicing*—issues of being together or being apart (for example, the child begins to experiment with distance, being near and far, or the child performs a newly emergent verbal skill, naming an object that is a distance away); *rapprochement*—issues of being in control or being controlled by someone else (for example, the child wanders away and wants his parent to follow, or the child protests having to follow parental expectations); and *object constancy*—issues of being dependent or being autonomous (for example, the child enjoys playing quietly in his room, insisting on being "on his own") (Mahler 1972a, 1972b).

In his play, Ben clearly struggles with issues of sameness and differentness. He is torn apart by conflict and cannot contain his own aggressive impulses. As a result, tension is pervasive and at least once interrupts the flow of the narrative. He attempts to portray the practicing issues of being together versus being apart in the battling soldiers, but that play segment is quickly followed by the depiction of injury, failure of protection, and destruction. Ben uses the presence of his therapist as a source of security, enabling him to portray these upsetting scenes. Conflictual segments are offset by Ben's attempts at self-soothing, using the autono-

mous activities of construction and ball play. Ben's concern with earlier relationship issues (differentiation, practicing) in the play narrative stands in
sharp contrast to his higher capacities for relationship, which can be
observed, for example, in his interactions with the therapist (reciprocal
play).

Structural analysis of the play activity examines component processes that
contribute to the structure of play activity. Play activity includes affective,
cognitive, narrative, and developmental components. None of these
components acts separately in the pragmatics of play activity.

How will the child use his play? What function does the play serve for
the child? Is he master of the play? Or, does the play itself become synonymous with his life? Where is the boundary between fantasy and reality? Or,
are there multiple boundaries between multiple realities and fantasies?
These are some of the questions to be explored in the chapters to come.

In chapters 2 to 5 a spectrum of coping–defensive strategies will be
described as they appear in play activity. The four *clusters* of coping–
defensive strategies are *adaptive* strategies, *conflicted* strategies, *rigid/
polarized* strategies, and *extreme anxiety/isolated* strategies. It is important to
note that in labeling these clusters of play strategies in this book the
emphasis is on the relationship of the child to himself (intrapsychic) and to
others (interpersonal). This is a diversion from the original CPTI use of the
diagnostic categories normal, neurotic, borderline, psychotic to describe
play activity. The change in designation is meant to clarify that the play
strategies used by the child are not necessarily isomorphic with the overall
mental state of the child. Clinically, play activity cannot be understood as
necessarily diagnostic of the child's psychological state. The child may be
playing out a dilemma, recalling a memory, trying out different actions or
narratives, without other direct implications. The only way to ascertain the
diagnostic meaning of the play activity would be to conduct a complete
evaluation of the child and his family, play activity being only one
component of that evaluation.

The next four chapters describe play activity profiles in reference to
specific children who present with clinical issues. The question of the
meaning of the play activity profile will be considered separately for each
child. Is it possible to have pathological components within the play profile

of an adaptive player? Is it possible to have adaptive components within the play profile of an extremely anxious/isolated child? Chapter 2 begins to explore these questions by describing the function of adaptive coping–defensive strategies observed in the child at play.

The Adaptive Player

Erik Erikson (1977) has described the microcosm block structure constructed by a very active 5-year-old black boy, Robert. Invited into the
playroom, Robert immediately constructs a high, symmetrical, and
well-balanced structure in the middle of the table. He distributes toy
vehicles on the floors and ledges of the block construction. He then groups
all the animals together in a scene beside the tower; a snake is the center of
the animals' attention. Next, he chooses his first human figure, a black boy
whom he places at the very top of the building. Other dolls are put lying
supine on the vehicles, and some authoritative male figures (doctor,
policeman, old man) are put on top of them, facing up. The remaining
human dolls stand in a half circle around the animal figures, arms uplifted in
some excitement. Robert's narrative is short and concise: "Cars come to the
house. The lion bites the snake, wiggles his tail. The monkey and the kitten
try to kill the snake. People come to watch. Little one (black boy) on the
roof, is where smoke comes out (p. 32).

Erikson comments that the play scene is definitely "boyish" and
advanced for Robert's chronological age. He points to the unique feature of
the dolls' outstretched arms and notes that the block structure itself
resembles a standing body with arms outstretched. The black boy doll is at
the very top, or head, of this "body" structure. Robert's teachers have noted
that he often did an unusual thing in class. With a detached smile, he would
dance a two-step around the room with his arms outstretched sideways.
When commended by the teacher for the gracefulness of his dancing,
Robert would reply, "Yes, but my brain is no good." Erikson connects
Robert's words with his actions and sees as the essence of the play his hope

to bring his body and mind together and have them work as one unit. According to Erikson, in this play activity Robert is observed creating a drama surrounding his block structure in which he works through conflict regarding his deficient self-confidence and strivings for efficacy. He performs a new beginning, confesses, engages in joyful self-expression, exercises newly mastered skills, and transforms affective representation from anger to hopefulness. Maybe, as Erikson suggests, there is a chance of his growing up to be loved and lovable.

By constructing a story about his block structure, Robert is able to understand affectively (to understand with feelings) the drama of his own existence. This story is constructed by Robert himself, along with the structure of blocks. He interacts with other people, toys, and blocks to make his statement. The story incorporates painful feelings of despair (smoke) in a strong assertive effort to resolve differences within the self and become an integrated person. Activity within the microcosm, the small world developed with the child's imagination, encompasses the play activity that makes this forward movement possible.

Adaptation, then, is synonymous with playfulness. It is the uninterrupted, forward-moving, joyful effort towards mastery referred to by Robert White (1959) as competence motivation and by J. McV. Hunt (1965) as intrinsic motivation. From a similar perspective, Joseph Lichtenberg (1989) considered symbolic play to be an attempt at problem-solving, a derivative of the exploratory–assertive motivational system. While playing, the child explores adaptational possibilities that will lead to change, eventuating in increased feelings of confidence and competence. The concept of coping includes those efforts to deal with the challenges of life. Lois Barclay Murphy (1962) and her associates studied the characteristics of children who cope with difficulty successfully. They examined the quality of resilience among children who could actively engage their surroundings, accepting good and bad experiences as part of everyday reality and striving towards maintaining optimal integration, security, and comfort. From their studies they obtained a profile of "good copers," who could tolerate frustration, handle anxiety, and ask for help when they needed it. Their work has been extended by others, such as Anthony & Cohler (1987), who have studied the "invulnerable child."

In play activity, adaptive strategies form a cluster of related activities that share the propensity to lead towards adaptation. This cluster of adaptive strategies is closely linked to efforts by the child to cope constructively with the challenges of his environment, and to respond to these challenges with resilience. The adaptive strategies are future-oriented, problem-solving, and directed towards the transformation of toxic anxiety into hope. Traumatic anxiety that can be paralyzing and overwhelming is harnessed in the pursuit of constructive goals. It is the counter-toxic signaling function of anxiety that prepares the child so he can anticipate the upsetting event. Anticipation has the potential function of inoculating the child against trauma. Preparation and foresight enable the child to plan and maximize his potential for flexibility and self-regulation.

Adaptive strategies rarely exist independently of other more defensive strategies. As Lois Murphy and her colleagues suggested, coping is a combination of adaptation and defense. The child may use defense mechanisms as part of the overall coping effort. Thus, if change happens too quickly, or conflict is too much to bear, a defense mechanism may assist the child's efforts to cope, by dividing a complex situation into manageable parts or repressing the excessive threat and focusing on what can be mastered. The child at play presents an amalgam of adaptive and defensive strategies. Attributes of some children can potentially contribute to adaptive outcomes. These characteristics include a deep capacity for sensuous delight and gratification, a capacity for nonverbal interpersonal communication that can contribute to a genuine interpersonal relationship, a capacity for resourceful manipulation and problem-solving leading to play activity, and a capacity for representation and symbolization of disturbing experiences and fantasies (Murphy & Moriarty 1976).

Selma Fraiberg (1959) described a little boy, Tony, with generalized fears of the strange, the unfamiliar, and the unknown. His approach to coping with these feelings was to investigate the problem. If he could somehow find how something worked, he could understand the causes for events and feel in control of his fear. At age two, his favorite toy was a pocket-sized screwdriver he carried with him everywhere. He used this tool to unhinge doors and disassemble tables and chairs. When his parents put a stop to this research, he became furious. Warnings only seemed to increase his need to locate the source of danger and to find out "why." As he grew older, not only did he want to take dangerous things apart, he also wanted to make them work again. At age four years, he had an emergency appendectomy. Relatives wanted to bring him toys, but he asked for an old alarm clock that did not work and set about repairing it, just as the doctors had taken him apart and then put him together again. Thus, Tony used a well-established sublimation, including mechanical exploration and construction, to overcome a frightening experience. As he matured, Tony continued his scientific interests and eventually became a physicist. The interests expressed in play activity enabled Tony to cope with trauma and to exceed performance of children of his chronological age. Tony's style of coping while playing later became generalized to a style of coping with life. In these later life sequelae, adaptation continued to predominate over defense in leading to a "path towards mastery" (Murphy 1962).

Adaptive Strategies Used By the Child at Play

The Children's Play Therapy Instrument (Kernberg, Chazan, & Normandin 1997) enumerates and defines nine adaptive strategies that can be observed in a child's play. Each of these adaptive strategies is conceptualized as belonging to a larger cluster of adaptive play behaviors. In what follows, these adaptive strategies are first defined individually, each with its implied narrative expression (Kernberg 1994, 1989). Two clinical cases are then analyzed, showing how children employ selected strategies in a predominantly adaptive stance while playing.

Adaptation

The play activity expresses an effective accommodation to given circumstances; that is, it has a reality component.

"Let's make the best best use of what we have."

Anticipation

The play activity reflects planning for the future. Attention is focused on what will happen next and may involve preparation, expectation, apprehension, or a combination of these feelings and attitudes.

"I'll think it over ahead of time and be better prepared."

Problem-Solving

The play activity includes a trial-and-error component or a planned, systematic effort to clarify something that is unclear.

> "If I take my time and think carefully, there must be a solution to this problem."

Suppression

In the play activity, conflicts or stress are dealt with by intentionally avoiding thinking or talking about them.

> "I'll try my best not to think about it, and come back to it later."

Sublimation

An activity gratifying an impulse or wish is transformed into socially acceptable and creative activity.

> "I'd like to make a mess, but instead I'll work with the clay to make a work of art."

Altruism

The play activity involves concern for fulfilling the needs of others instead of the child's own needs in a socially acceptable way; it may be considered a form of sublimation.

> "I would be happy if you would take what I have."

Affiliation

The child plays that he belongs to a group of people by sharing activities, attributes, or a common goal (including asking for help).

> "I want to be doing what the others are doing, or they can join with me."

Identification

The child plays at being similar or identical to another person or character, in one or more attributes, roles, feelings, or behaviors.

> "I am like him and he is like me."

Humor

The play activity is perceived as funny because of incongruity, exaggeration, or unexpected events, seen as amusing and pleasurable. It is accompanied by or results in laughter.

"I can see what is going on from different points of view. This is fun!"

Clinical Case: Carla and the "Evoked Companion"

Play activity develops within the context of relationship. It may emerge from a child's relationship with himself, with others, and/or with objects, fantasized or real. When a needed object or person is not immediately present, the child may use a substitute for the thing that is missing. Alternatively, the child may use his imagination to evoke the unavailable other. The presence of these "evoked" fantasy objects is often indicated by a nonverbal signal, changed attitude, or gesture of recognition. These evoked representations provide a basis for expanded recognition of the self by the self, of the self by others, and of others by the self. They provide an extended vocabulary for interaction and conjuring up possible worlds. In the case of Carla, recognition of the child's subjective experience by the therapist provides a basis for the integration of negative feelings into a common bond of trust. The security of being understood provides a context for the development of adaptive play.

Carla, four and a half years old, was referred by a foster care agency for mental health intervention because of oppositionalism evidenced in temper tantrums and non-compliance with her adoptive mother's requests. In addition, the adopting mother needed assistance in limit-setting. Carla had been adopted at one year and six months of age by a 52-year-old woman with two older children of her own, who were no longer living in the home. Carla's DSM IV diagnosis at the time of referral was Reactive Attachment Disorder of Early Childhood, as evidenced in a lack of selectivity in choice of attachment figures and a highly ambivalent attitude towards caregivers.

Little of Carla's early history was available. Carla had been neglected by her natural mother, who was profoundly deaf and mute. She weighed 5 pounds 8 ounces at birth. When she was placed in foster care at 11 months of age, she was undernourished and underweight. There was no evidence of drug exposure in the birth parent or child. According to the adoptive mother's report, Carla had no speech at 13 months. She said "Mama" at 18 months, put two words together at two years, and at two and a half years was speaking sentences. Tested on the Stanford-Binet at four years of age, Carla achieved an intelligence quotient of 110. There was some discrepancy between verbal and nonverbal skills: verbal skills were in the low average range, while visual-motor skills were in the high average range.

The vignette to be described is excerpted from the 15th session of ongoing treatment, which included weekly play sessions for Carla and weekly counseling sessions for the adoptive mother. Difficulties in the treatment alliance were finally ameliorating at the time of this session. Carla and her mother were initially negative to the current therapist. They missed their previous therapist, though they had both known before beginning treatment that the therapists were in training and would rotate out of the clinic at the end of the school year. All patients were apprised of the limitations imposed by the training schedule before beginning treatment. The adoptive mother gave various reasons to account for her own uneven pattern of attendance.

Following is a verbatim transcript from videotape.

(Therapist is holding doll that contains a music box in it; the music is playing.)

Therapist:	You didn't say hello to her today! She was waiting for you!
Therapist:	*(For doll)* Wah…waah!
Carla:	Hello, hello. *(Blows whistle in a large pink plastic hammer at the doll)*
Therapist:	She's scared. She's shaking. *(Therapist shakes doll)*
Carla:	*(Laughs in excited, shrill, high-pitched laughter and repeats the loud noise directed at the doll, then continues shrill bursts of laughter)*
Therapist:	She's scared. She's shaking. She's scared of loud noises. *(Shakes doll)*
Carla:	*(Continues to laugh in guttural staccato bursts and gets ready to blow at doll again)*

Therapist:	You want to scare her, she's hiding. She's going to hide because she is scared of loud noises.
Carla:	*(Continues to lean forward and make loud whistling noise at doll)*
Therapist:	You like scaring her. I guess you want to make her very scared.
Carla:	*(Staccato laughter)*
Therapist:	Does Carla ever get scared? I guess it's very scary to be scared. *(Therapist sits up doll and positions it toward Carla)*
Carla:	*(Approaches doll, leans forward and regards intently)*
Therapist:	*(As Carla approaches doll)* What are you looking at?... at her eyes?
Carla:	No.

(C. picks up glass paperweight, shakes it, turns it upside down and regards the snow falling inside the glass globe. The doll is situated behind the paperweight. C. lifts the paperweight above her head and gazes upwards at the falling snow, spellbound, a smile lighting up her face. There is a long, protracted moment of direct gaze up at the glass paperweight and the falling snow. *This moment seems to evoke for C. shared feelings of goodness and beauty. Her upward gaze suggests the posture of an infant looking up adoringly at her caregiver.)*

Therapist:	*(Speaking for doll)* Can I watch? I want to see the snow.
Carla:	*(Shows paperweight to doll)*
Therapist:	*(Speaking for doll)* Oh, isn't that pretty?
Carla:	Yeah.
Therapist:	*(Therapist maneuvers doll to follow path of paperweight as Carla lowers it. Therapist is speaking for doll)* All the glitter!

(Music continues. Doll and Carla regard paperweight together.)

Carla:	*(Winds up the music box. Excitedly)* I turned it on! *(meaning the music)*
Therapist:	*(Lies doll down)* She's falling asleep. *(Carla approaches with whistle)* You want to wake her up again.

Therapist:	*(Speaking for doll)* You keep waking me up and scaring me Ms. Carla.
Carla:	*(Makes loud whistling noise and hits doll with hammer several times)*
Therapist:	*(Speaking for doll)* That hurt! That hurt a lot!
Carla:	I want you to sleep.
Therapist:	*(Speaking for doll)* I don't want to sleep! I want to stay up!
Carla:	*(Continues to blow whistle and hit doll)*
Therapist:	OK *(Takes whistle, setting limit. Doll goes to sleep again, then wakes up)*
Carla:	*(Gleefully laughing, picks up cymbals and bangs)*
Therapist:	*(Speaking for doll)* I don't want to sleep with all of this banging. *(Makes doll dance)* It doesn't sound like music. It sounds like banging!
Carla:	*(Begins making rhythmic beats)* I'll dance with her.

(Carla gives cymbals to Therapist. Therapist plays cymbals, watches C. dance with doll. Carla winds up music box in doll.)

Therapist:	Are you teaching her to dance? What is that? *(Carla is showing the crystal globe to the doll)*

The play activity segment ends as Carla turns her attention to searching for a different doll and setting up a new scene. This new scene will be around toilet training where the doll performs successfully.

DESCRIPTIVE ANALYSIS OF THE PLAY ACTIVITY

Carla's play activity was categorized as fantasy play. The play activity occurred entirely within the microsphere, the sphere of toys and small replicas of real objects. Carla repeatedly frightened and hit her doll. The repetitive nature of the hitting suggested it might depict in part traumatic punishment Carla has experienced. On the other hand, the subsequent evocation of good feelings suggested the experience of coming together with a loving person. It was unclear what elicited this change in feelings.

Perhaps it was triggered by feelings of warmth and acceptance conveyed by the therapist, or perhaps her affectionate feelings occurred in response to the soothing auditory stimulus of the melody or the visible image of softly falling snow. As her play continued, Carla's negative resistant feelings for her therapist and toys were certainly giving way to more positive feelings of confident expectations.

We can only speculate as to the meaning of our observations. The doll, formerly the recipient of punishment, was invited to join Carla in her dance. The movement of the dance was Carla's expressive response to the evoked good object, the glass globe containing the softly falling snow. These good feelings were, in turn, shared with the doll/child. Then the doll was transformed from a bad child to a companion who could join in and enjoy the fun of dancing.

All of this play took place under the watchful eye of the therapist. Although the therapist initiated the play activity by inviting Carla's attention to the doll, Carla quickly responded with her own repetitive theme of punishing the doll. The therapist repeatedly facilitated the play, particularly by verbalizing a running account of the play activity and its consequences. It was Carla, however, who found the good moment. These good feelings seem to emanate from deep within Carla. As she looked upward with a shining countenance at the sight of the falling snow, the therapist echoed and resonated to "all of the glitter," and the music continued to play in the background. Carla eagerly reflected on her own sense of agency, saying "I turned it on," referring to the music box inside the doll. All three protagonists (Carla, the therapist, and the doll) were able to bask together in the warmth of this shared moment.

When she first turned to the paperweight, Carla left the shared focus with doll and therapist to evoke a separate subjective reality. She was then able to share her discovery with the therapist and doll. She emerged from enmeshment with the terror of punitive attack to literally turn aside and move away, allowing her glance to turn upward to a pleasurable encounter. This shift in relatedness progressed from shared interaction to the evocation of a new presence and a return to shared interaction. The middle step was also an interaction, but with an evoked companion. In this way, the pleasurable moment became integrated into experience with the originally bad doll.

The emergence of this evoked experience occurred as a solitary event of playing alone while in the presence of the therapist and doll. The integration of these two experiences, shared and solitary/aware, within the play sequence was a marker of therapeutic progress. The therapist's facilitation of this integration occurred first with her attunement and compliance with Carla's insistence that the doll go to sleep and then with her suggestion that the doll did not like the loud banging of the cymbals. Carla reciprocated by modifying her banging into a soft rhythmic beat. Regulation between the players shifted from defiance to cooperation and compliance. Carla gave the therapist the cymbals to continue the soft rhythmic beat, so that she was free to dance with the doll.

The play activity was ended by Carla, who turned her attention to a different doll. Carla began a pre-play segment by setting the stage for play activity around the theme of toilet training.

STRUCTURAL ANALYSIS OF THE PLAY ACTIVITY

Affective Components

Feelings expressed by Carla while playing fluctuated between obvious pleasure and overt distress. While the spectrum of affects was wide in its variation between these two discrete points, it was also constricted, as the emotional tone did not fluctuate widely but remained organized around these two emotional states. Carla proceeded abruptly from expressing anger to expressing awe and delight. She did not modulate her feelings, and the transition between emotional states was always abrupt. Feelings expressed by Carla as she played included aggression, anger, anxiety, curiosity, awe, and pleasure, and they were always appropriate to the content of her play. She was somewhat positive in her feelings for the therapist, although at times she was shrill and oppositional and at other moments gentle and loving. Her therapist was usually warm and at times firm and directive.

Cognitive Components

Carla represented several roles in her play, including the doll, herself as partner to the doll and the evoked companion, and the therapist as playmate and musicmaker. Most of the play activity was simple collaborative play, with the doll as her partner, but the last moments of the play were complex collaborative play, that included herself and the doll dancing, with the therapist as musicmaker. Both Carla and the doll underwent voluntary transformations: the doll was transformed from bad to good, and Carla from aggressor to playmate. The doll and the evoked companion were represented in a magical/fantasy style, while Carla represented herself in a realistic style.

Narrative Components

The theme of Carla's play revolved around caregiving; topics of the play including punishment and beauty. The quality of relationships within the play narrative fluctuated between malevolent control and dependence. Carla was primarily silent during her play; she depended upon actions and gestures to communicate. One exception was an intense, pivotal moment when she recognized her own ability to make the music box work. The therapist's language included verbalization of the role of the doll and talking during the play describing the play.

It was particularly poignant that for Carla auditory channels played such an important role in her play (the music box). As a very young child she was probably often startled by her deaf and mute parents who were not attuned to her auditory needs. Resolution of the abusive relationship in the play took place through visual channels (the falling snow), which in Carla's earliest years probably offered opportunities for comforting merger experiences.

Developmental Components

The developmental level of the play activity was somewhat immature for Carla's chronological age. Particularly notable was the sparse use of language. The gender identity of the play activity was predominantly feminine, as she played at caregiving to her doll. Separation–individuation issues represented in the play were predominantly the ambivalence of the rapprochement phase and some beginning suggestion of constancy in the resolution of the play theme. At first Carla teased, hurt, and startled the doll, yet at the same time she allowed the therapist to comfort the doll. Then, as the play ended, Carla invited the doll to dance and shared with her the crystal globe (paperweight). Carla's interaction with her therapist mani-

fested several levels of social development, including solitary (aware), reciprocal, and cooperative interactions.

FUNCTIONAL ANALYSIS OF THE PLAY ACTIVITY

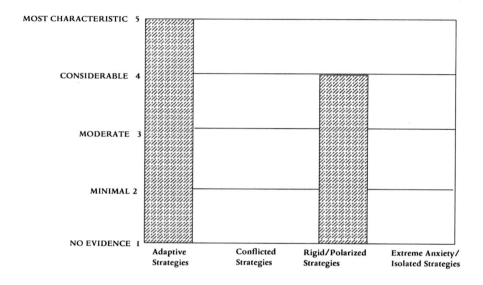

Figure 2.1 Carla's Coping–Defensive Strategies

Carla's coping–defensive strategies throughout her course of treatment are
shown graphically in Figure 2.1. Adaptive coping strategies were most
characteristic of her play activity. In her doll play and in interaction with her
therapist Carla was observed to use the coping strategies of *affiliation, identification* and *sublimation*. Affiliation occurred in Carla's relatedness to the
therapist and her connection (although initially abusive) to the doll. Identification was evident in her following the lead taken by the therapist in the
play and in her affection for the doll at the end of the play. Carla consented
to having the doll be comforted and watch the falling snow, and finally
taught the doll how to dance. In the last activity she was enacting the caring
role previously enacted by the therapist. Carla was not only identifying with
the beneficent attitude of the therapist; by inference she was also identifying

with the abused doll, who was rehabilitated. Sublimation occurred when instead of teasing the doll Carla taught her. In both instances Carla took the more powerful role, but as teacher she formed a bond with the doll through caring. This change in play enactment suggested Carla no longer experiences an overwhelming need to tease the doll in order to feel related to her. Carla was unaware her enjoyment of the dancing was in any way related to her earlier feelings. At these moments Carla's play activity emerged spontaneously and joyfully, with an independence of its own.

While there was no evidence of conflict in this segment of Carla's play, there was considerable evidence of rigid/polarized defensive strategies. These strategies included *idealization, devaluation,* and *identification with the aggressor;* these strategies will be discussed in detail in Chapter 4. Observation revealed that Carla's play behaviors and affective states were organized in two very different patterns, one loving, the other attacking. This division into polarized patterns was pervasive in Carla's narrative and reflected her subjective experience. No isolated defense strategies were observed in Carla's play; Carla was always aware of herself as playing.

The organization of Carla's coping/defense strategies into two distinctive affective states—aggressive and loving—suggested that transient dissociative states were reflected in Carla's play activity. In the context of Carla's play, the dissociative response was communicated without the added toxic effects of real-life trauma. This organization within the play functioned as communication to the observer of a reenactment of the traumatic event, as well as an attempt to gain mastery over the frightening experience. In this instance, Carla was enabled to repair the injured parties (herself and the doll) through shared movement and love. As L. B. Murphy (1962) observed, adaptive play is never free of elements of conflict and defense. It was the completed reparation that categorizes this play activity segment as adaptive.

Clinical Case: Kate and the "Land of the Unwanted"

Kate was a nine-year-old girl in the fourth grade. She was described by her mother as a loner with no friends and very stubborn. One of her teachers felt that Kate was "trying to escape" by always keeping her nose in a book. Kate's mother and father divorced when Kate was two years old. Kate's mother remarried and had two additional children. She commented that adding to the family had had a negative effect on Kate, who for the first six years of her life had had her mother's exclusive attention. Her mother could not resolve her feelings of guilt and alternately blamed herself, her husband, and her ex-husband and then blamed Kate for not being able to care for herself.

Kate, a bright, lively, creative, diminutive young girl, often came to sessions dressed sloppily in the same paint-stained leggings, sneakers, and long top. She was usually happy, cooperative, and assertive. Kate could focus easily and made good eye contact. Using humor, she was able to laugh often and easily. Over the course of the first year of treatment, it became clear that Kate had tremendous difficulty expressing any negative feelings. She always wanted to be perceived as sweet and compliant, and she valued perfection highly. A reflection of the two sides of this conflict was seen in a drawing of a man whom she described as "really nice. He's never mean and never gets mad." The man was holding a report card with all As on it. The therapist commented that the man must be imaginary, "because everybody gets mad and is mean sometimes." Kate responded, "Well, you haven't met his friend yet." She then drew a man who she said was mean all of the time and failed all of his classes. She used a tissue to erase both men and commented that they live together in the tissue.

Kate was frequently disappointed by the adults in her life, who would tell her one thing and do another. She was very conflicted about coming to treatment and insecure about the therapist's dependability and trustworthiness. Blending her worst fears with her fondest hopes, Kate made up a game called the Magic Box. A character, designated by Kate as the therapist, finds a Magic Box. The Magic Box holds three containers, each one filled with transformation powders. Kate posed questions to the therapist: Would she use the powder immediately? Or would she find out everything she could about the Magic Box—who used it, how it works, whether it is good or evil, or, would she not want to do anything with the box and throw it away? Scarcely concealed are Kate's concerns about what kind of person the therapist is, whether she can be trusted, and what it is the therapist might transform her into.

Perhaps reflecting this uncertainty, Kate did not engage in fantasy play during the first six months of treatment, despite her obvious gift for creativity. Instead, even the smallest disclosure was followed by withdrawal and her choosing to play a board game appropriate for her age, such as *Clue* or *Monopoly*. Some of Kate's expressiveness emerged as spontaneous poetry. In other instances, her longings appeared in the guise of playfulness, during the dialogue of non-play.

An Excerpt From the Seventh Treatment Session

Kate was brought to the session by her father. There was considerable discussion about conflicting activities and the difficulty of arranging appointment times. Kate willingly relinquished swimming (a favorite activity) in order to keep her appointments.

Upon entering the playroom, Kate volunteered that she had composed a poem and asked if the therapist would like to hear it. The therapist replied she would like that very much.

Kate:	Sleep *I lie in my little bed, a small pillow beneath my head* *It is hard to say when sleep will come my way.*
Therapist:	That's great. What made you think of it?
Kate:	I guess because Johnny [her stepfather] got a new computer and he went to the Disney site. We are on the Internet now.
Therapist:	Cool. *(Pause)* Do you ever have trouble falling asleep?
Kate:	No, not really—I like to stay awake and read. But once I'm asleep, I sleep like a log. I read until my mom makes me go to sleep.
Therapist:	Do you have your own room?
Kate:	No, I have a bunk bed with Emmy on the bottom, and Ben is in the crib.
Therapist:	So, you wouldn't be able to stay up reading because of them?
Kate:	Well, no, because I have a little reading light.
Therapist:	What do you like to read?

Kate:	Science fiction mostly. *A Wrinkle in Time* is my favorite book.
Therapist:	What did you like about it?
Kate:	That they travel to other dimensions. In one of them Meg goes to this other world to save her dad and bring him back home. In another one she says, "I love you." It breaks the spell. She's young in the book. Yeah, about twelve.
Therapist:	So, you really like to read.
Kate:	Sometimes it distracts me, though, when I'm in school, I can't concentrate on math because it's like I sometimes feel like the characters in the books.
Therapist:	In what ways?
Kate:	Well, if the character has an English accent, I start to think in an English accent.
Therapist:	Ah, so—it's *how* they talk, not what they say.
Kate:	Well, sometimes what they say.
Therapist:	Like what?
Kate:	Like I start to think—well, once I had a dream that I had a magic dress, and when I wore it, it made this train go anywhere I wanted to.
Therapist:	When did you dream that?
Kate:	Oh, about a year ago.
Therapist:	Well, what do you think about it?
Kate:	Well—I never wear dresses, so it was weird. But maybe because I had a nightdress on in my sleep. Do you ever have dreams you remember?
Therapist:	Yes.
Kate:	Could you tell me one?
Therapist:	Sure. I had a dream when I was little about a camp and I didn't like it.

Kate:	Oh, I had this dream the other night that my mom was a dodo bird and I was a bird. And all the birds were flying, and I couldn't fly—I thought, my mom is a dodo bird, so, why can't I fly?
Therapist:	Could your mom fly?
Kate:	I don't think so.
Therapist:	Both dreams had to do with going somewhere—either flying, or taking the magic train. Where would you go, if you could?
Kate:	Antarctica.
Therapist:	How come?
Kate:	I like the cold and I'd see penguins.
Therapist:	I don't think anyone would be there. What would you do?
Kate:	Probably build a igloo. But, I could always come back!

The session ended with a game of *Monopoly*. The therapist and Kate decided to maintain a tally sheet, so they could keep playing from session to session.

The opening poem barely concealed Kate's deep longings. She was longing to let go, to relax and to sleep—to let her imagination wander. But first she had to feel secure enough to relinquish wakefulness. Uncertainty imperiled her ever being able to reach this desired state as she lacked a reliable nurturing relationship. This dialogue between Kate and her therapist was non-play, although it contained imaginary elements.

Kate liked to read about travel to faraway places. It was a dress, an outer garment with magical powers, that enabled her to go wherever she wanted to. She dreamt that both she and her mom were dodo birds. They shared a common trait: although they were both birds, neither of them could fly. Was this an allusion to feeling stuck and unable to let go?

Kate wished that she were someone else. When she read about a character, she almost became the character. She twinned with her mother, the immovable dodo bird. If she could fly, she would go to a very cold and isolated place, perhaps to flee from her feelings of discomfort and to search for the company of other birds who could not fly, the penguins. Most important of all, Kate asserted that although she took off to a cold climate, she could always return. This notion of the safety in return promoted the promise of secure reunion. The session ended with a play activity segment of game play. Kate and her therapist tallied up the results to assure the continuity of their relationship, expressed through the continuity in play activity and the return to future sessions.

Session at the End of the Sixth Month of Therapy

About mid-session, following a game of catch, Kate initiated a game of guessing words that were disguised in drawings. The therapist was sitting with her back to the board, and Kate gave her two dolls to hold. The therapist turned to face the board while she cradled and cooed to the dolls; she asked the dolls if they wanted to take a nap. Kate wrote the word "dolly." After the therapist guessed the word, Kate wrote in the corner of the board "You good mama."

Therapist:	She's a good mama?
Kate:	No, *you're* a good mama.

(The therapist writes the word "cuddle," and Kate writes the word "rest." The therapist writes the word "food," and Kate writes the word "happy.")

Kate:	OK, I'm tired. I'm going to go lie down. *(She lies down)*
Therapist:	We need a blanket, but we don't have one, so I'll cover you with animals. *(Kate giggles) (Therapist proceeds to clean up room)* Are you asleep yet?
Kate:	*(No answer)*
Therapist:	You must have been so tired, you didn't even need me to read one of your books to you.
Kate:	Oh, will you?
Therapist:	We don't have time today.
Kate:	Just a quick version of *Cinderella* and *Beauty and the Beast.*

The therapist complies with a two-minute synopsis, and the session ends.

DESCRIPTIVE ANALYSIS OF THE PLAY ACTIVITY

In this session Kate introduced a creative form of communication in which she replicated the paradigm of a game of catch in a new word game. Therapist and Kate took turns challenging each other to guess a word concealed in a visual image. The meaning communicated by the image was more than the image itself; there was something else concealed within it that contained another meaning. It followed that the therapist was not just playing at being a "mama"; the play concealed the shared reality for the child that at that moment the therapist has become the "good" mama. Therapist and child continued with reciprocal associations to the themes of nurturance and caregiving. Kate's wishes were barely concealed as she became "sleepy" and entered the longed-for state of being securely held. The therapist responded by tidying up, and Kate responded by "letting go" into silence. They ended with words, in shared familiar stories evoking a magical realm, and Kate departed.

This play activity segment was categorized as organized game play (catch) that developed into an original word game. Kate initiated the play activity, and it was consistently facilitated by the give and take of associations between therapist and child. There was no inhibition of the play activity. The play was ended by the therapist, because the session ended. Clearly, Kate would have liked to continue. The play took place primarily in the macrosphere (space of everyday objects), but there was some introduction of stuffed animals, items from the microsphere (space of toys and small objects).

STRUCTURAL ANALYSIS OF THE PLAY ACTIVITY

Affective Components

The overall hedonic tone of this play activity segment was obvious pleasure. As Kate wrote the word "happy" and lay down to rest, her feelings of fulfillment in the relationship seemed to come bursting through. Kate's spectrum of expressed feelings was narrow, with medium regulation and modification of affects. Her transitions between affective states were usually smooth; her affective tone was always appropriate to the content of the play. Feelings expressed by Kate while playing included pleasure and curiosity. The feelings expressed between therapist and child were consistently very positive.

Cognitive Components

Dyadic roles were represented; the therapist is the "good" mama, and Kate played at being her child. The two dolls did not take on specific identities, but they may have represented Kate's two half-siblings, whom she perceived to be getting the love and attention she wanted; when the therapist used the dolls as her children, Kate took the role as the therapist's child to be her own and set the dolls aside. The dyadic roles of mother and child remained stable, with no transformations in role occurring. Kate went along with the therapist's suggestion of using the stuffed animals as a blanket, which represented the substitution of one object for another. In accepting this substitution, Kate was also accepting the understanding that something else, or someone else, could be placed in the role of another through imagining. The implication for the therapist–patient relationship (transference) was implicit: "using our imagination (which Kate was reluctant to do initially) we can enact together your wishes for a caring relationship." In this symbolic play the animals (Kate's fantasy creatures) became a source of protection and the therapist became the "good" mama. The style of representation of objects and persons was consistently realistic.

Narrative Components

The topic of the play activity was game play and the "One Who Cares." The theme of the play activity was caregiving. The level of relationship portrayed in the narrative was dyadic; the quality of relationship portrayed in the narrative was dependent. Language was used by both Kate and her therapist to play with words and to verbalize their roles.

Developmental Components

Kate's choice of doll play and the unelaborated theme of the play were somewhat immature for her age. There was no development of characters. It was the evoked atmosphere of nurturance and caregiving that suffused the play with a warm glow. This affective expression alone was sufficient to complete the play activity, that expanded subsequently through the use of a word game. Kate hid her words within objects, just as she experienced in play that objects could hold hidden feelings. In our culture, the caregiving roles enacted by Kate and her therapist are traditionally associated with women. Receiving warmth and nurturance within the context of play, Kate was representing the oral receptive level of psychosexual development. Separation–individuation issues portrayed in the play activity included differentiation of little Kate from her mama, formation of a healthy symbiosis, and the beginning of practicing separation, as Kate played at going to sleep. The social level of interaction between Kate and her therapist was reciprocal and cooperative.

FUNCTIONAL ANALYSIS OF THE PLAY ACTIVITY

Adaptive strategies were most characteristic of this play activity. These strategies included *affiliation, identification* and *sublimation*. Kate was clearly related to her therapist and identified with her Mama's good caregiving, thus sublimating her need for a secure attachment by playing out a gratifying parent–child relationship. There was moderate use of conflictual strategies in the play activity, as Kate projected her needs into the role of being a younger and dependent child, thus employing both *projection* and *regression* within the role-play. No rigid/polarized strategies or strategies involving extreme anxiety/isolation were observed in the play activity.

This play activity segment was a transitional step on the way to fantasy play. The shared associations of therapist and child led to an enactment within the mother–child transference, where Kate seemed to be realizing her fondest wishes. In this session we observed Kate relax and begin to play at being the small child she longed to be. The regressive yearnings appeared within the safe confines of the play activity, diminishing fears that when the session ended she might not be able to return to everyday life with her family.

Second Session Following Return From Summer Interval: Eighth Month of Treatment

The session begins with a baseball game in semi-darkness initiated by Kate. Kate then turns on the lights and draws a picture of Fluffy the cat, which she then erases.

Kate:	Where do you think things go when they're erased? Do they go into the eraser, or stay on the board in some tiny form?
Therapist:	Hm-mm. What do you think?
Kate:	Hm-mm. They go to the Land of the Unwanted.
Therapist:	What's it like in the Land of the Unwanted?
Kate:	Well, it's nice because they can come alive again. And, because everyone there is unwanted, they feel good.
Therapist:	Because they have that in common?
Kate:	Yeah.
Therapist:	So, they are not lonely?
Kate:	No, not there. They were in the land of the real but they were unwanted—and there were too many people. Some were younger and crowded them out.
Therapist:	The younger ones came along and they, then, became unwanted?
Kate:	Yeah. So, in the Land of the Unwanted they have roommates they like—and there's a basketball hoop and a couch to sleep on and pictures on the wall and a garbage can. *(These are all objects actually in the therapy room)*
Therapist:	But nothing is unwanted, so what do they use it *(the garbage can)* for?
Kate:	…a hat at parties. And they are respected there and they get to play games—that game we play, Therapy. And there's a big sport called "Slaughter the Clock" and they have a competition to see who can kill the clock, because they hate the noisy clock. But I guess they need to tell time.
Therapist:	That clock sure is annoying. It's even unwanted in the Land of the Unwanted.
Kate:	*(Laughs)* And they have a box filled up with news stories and they get passes. Sometimes they go to the Land of

the Real, but there are no people, just trees and animals and ocean…and it's like a vacation for them. *(Draws picture of the Land of the Unwanted)*

Therapist: Looks a lot like this room.

Kate: Yeah, it does.

Therapist: It's time to leave.

DESCRIPTIVE ANALYSIS OF THE PLAY ACTIVITY

Kate began the session by initiating a game of baseball. Interestingly, she altered the perceptual state by lowering the lights, a suggestion that further modifications of external reality might follow. Kate then drew a picture of Fluffy the cat. Kate posed a question: "Where do things go when they are erased?" She was initiating a leap from concrete representation to the symbolic use of metaphor. She was concerned with the whereabouts of a visual image when it could no longer be seen. The question seemed clearly to refer to the loss of contact during the summer break. Was there any continuity of relationship during this time? Did relationships become fragmented into tiny bits, or absorbed into relationships with other people? What, if any, was the relationship between the remembered and the observed? Kate inferred that the reason for separation was rejection; reparation was when they become alive again in therapy, "the Land of the Unwanted." The common bond in this domain was the experience of having been rejected, thrown away like refuse that was no longer needed. Again, this was a barely concealed reference to Kate's own experience of rejection following the remarriage of her mother and the birth of two younger siblings. Even the garbage could be useful, as a hat. The dreaded object was the relentless clock, telling time and tying fantasy to reality in an inevitable way. When Kate returned to the Land of the Real, she found no people to hurt her or retaliate, only the restful scenes of nature. Kate left her fantasy world in a drawing as the session came to a close. Clearly, Kate was beginning to absorb the pattern of therapy sessions as she enacted the coming and going aspects of separation and reunion, and the coming and going to and from the realm of shared play activity.

The therapist and Kate both facilitated the emergence and continuity of this play activity, in which there was no inhibition. Play was ended by the therapist, because the session was ending. The play activity took place within a fantasy microsphere constructed by Kate.

STRUCTURAL ANALYSIS OF THE PLAY ACTIVITY

Affective Components

As in earlier therapy sessions, the overall hedonic tone was obviously pleasurable for both therapist and child. Here, however, the spectrum of affects expressed was wide, including expressions of pleasure, curiosity, anger, sadness, and aloofness. Kate regulated expression of her feelings well; the transitions between her feeling states were consistently smooth. Kate's affective tone was always appropriate to the content of the play. The feelings between therapist and child were consistently positive.

Cognitive Components

The level of role-play represented in the play was complex, as Kate took a leap to become the narrator of her story. There was also minimal evidence of beginning role-play, when Kate drew a picture of her main character, Fluffy the cat. Roles represented (the people who go to the Land of the Unwanted) underwent voluntary transformation as persons who were first rejected are then valued. This change may have been more apparent than real. The people were the same people, but they appeared vastly different depending upon how they were valued by others. Although the transformation may not have been complete, the drastic change in valuation (with change in place) resonated with the trauma encountered by Kate with the birth of her half-siblings. Visual representation of playthings, animals, and persons remained consistent, as all of them appeared the same in both locations. Play objects were used realistically in the play (an eraser was used to erase, a clock to tell time). The style of representation of the characters in the play was predominantly magical, as they existed in both realms of fantasy and the real world.

Narrative Components

The topic of Kate's playing was travel. The themes of her play activity were belonging and exclusion, separation and reunion. The play activity portrayed two groups, each group functioning as a collective unit, resulting in the dynamic of an accepted versus a rejected group. Relationships portrayed within the play narrative were manifestly autonomous, with an undercurrent of dependency. How the people felt about themselves depended upon the domain in which they resided. However, the movement of coming and going suggested a veneer of autonomy. Both child and therapist used language to express themselves within the metaphor of play.

Developmental Components

Kate's play activity, given the level of its abstraction, was somewhat advanced for her age. The metaphor was not only abstract but also had an ironic edge in barely concealing its intent. There was no predominance in the gender identity of the play. Kate's play used masked symbols for self-expression, a clear latency-age achievement (Sarnoff 1976). Separation–individuation issues in the play reflected concerns of the practicing phase, as the characters came and went between lands and between states of being alive and being erased. Social interaction between Kate and her therapist while she was playing was consistently reciprocal.

FUNCTIONAL ANALYSIS OF THE PLAY ACTIVITY

Adaptive strategies were most characteristic in Kate's play. These adaptive strategies included *sublimation, affiliation, identification,* and *humor.* Kate's identification with her therapist was seen in her choice of an "elsewhere" that was curiously isomorphic with clinic surroundings. Affiliation was reflected in her association of this magical land as a place where people are accepted for who they are. Kate's choice of metaphor gave her freedom to explore negative affects, not observed previously. This resolution of conflict through fantasy play was a good example of the use of sublimation and humor.

Kate was clearly aware that she was playing. The relationship between the two lands was abstract, yet they retained concrete elements of Kate's everyday experience. The Real Land sounded curiously like the vacation spot from which she had returned, with "no people, just trees, animals, and ocean." Kate seemed to have missed her therapist, while enjoying the surroundings of the beach. The clock and other objects, although part of the Land of the Unwanted, remind us of the playroom and the therapist's ending of the session when time runs out. Kate preserved for herself a representation of the therapy room and its objects, a depiction of her own inner life and how much of the therapy she has taken in. She has been given a chance to feel alive again, no longer "crowded out" by younger people. Kate's story only thinly veiled her feelings of rejection following the birth of her two younger half-siblings.

Conflictual strategies were also moderately evident in Kate's play activity. These conflictual strategies included *avoidance, reaction formation, projection,* and *intellectualization.* Kate chose to avoid relationships in the everyday world and to create a magical world that reversed the pain of living. She created an imaginary world that was the diametric opposite of her family experience. Although this conflict was successfully contained within play activity, it represented a solution using inversion in fantasy. By representing the opposite, Kate gave us an understanding of what she was striving to avoid. She projected her wishes onto a world of her own creation, using her intellect to imagine how this world might come true.

In this session, there was no evidence of rigid/polarized or extreme anxiety/isolated strategies in Kate's play activity.

Next Session, Later That Same Week

Kate:	*(Offers therapist a gummy bear)* Most grown-ups think these are too sweet. Do you want one?
Therapist:	Do you think I'll like it?
Kate:	I don't know. Do you like sweets?
Therapist:	Yeah.
Kate:	Here's a piece.
Therapist:	Mmm—good!
Kate:	You want more?
Therapist:	No, thanks.
Kate:	I got these at lunch with my friends. *(To stuffed animals)* Fluffy, Fluffy, how are you? Hi, Mr. Bunny! *(Acting as Mr. Bunny)* I'm hungry. *(As Kate)* You're hungry. Do you want some food? *(As Mr. Bunny)* Yes, please. I'd like some carrots.

(The therapist gets three orange markers and gives them to Mr. Bunny)

Kate:	*(As Mr. Bunny)* Chomp, chomp, chomp. I want some more.
Therapist:	How come bunny's so hungry?
Kate:	*(As Mr. Bunny)* I haven't eaten in a while.
Therapist:	How come?
Kate:	*(As Mr. Bunny)* Because I wasn't hungry.

(Therapist and Kate switch roles, with Kate playing Fluffy the Cat and the therapist being Mr. Bunny)

Kate:	Fluffy is hungry, too, but he's going to get his sardines and caviar. He gets to have a little piece of caviar every so often.
Therapist:	He can't have as much as he wants?
Kate:	No, because then he'd run out.
Therapist:	It must be hard. Don't you want to eat all the caviar, sometimes?
Kate:	*(As Fluffy)* No. It's okay, I have lots of sardines.
Therapist:	*(As Mr. Bunny)* Fluffy, do you have to go out and get your own food?
Kate:	*(As Fluffy)* Oh, no. I have lots of friends, like Mr. Raccoon and Bear who bring me scraps they find.
Therapist:	*(As Mr. Bunny)* I remember when I was little my mother would feed me. Now I feed myself.
Kate:	*(As Fluffy)* Ohhh, how come, Bunny? Where's your mommy?
Therapist:	*(As Mr. Bunny)* She's not always around. I was looking for her the other day, and I found her talking to Squirrel, but she didn't see me.
Kate:	*(As Fluffy)* Why didn't you tell her you were hungry?
Therapist:	*(As Mr. Bunny)* I don't know.

Kate:	*(As Kate)* Okay, let's bring Mommy Bunny in as this pillow.
Kate:	*(As Mommy Bunny)* Hi, Bunny. I'm here. Here are some carrots for you. And if you *ever* need me, I'll be in Bunker 38.
Therapist:	*(As Mr. Bunny)* Okay.
Therapist:	*(As Panda)* I'm hungry.
Kate:	*(As Fluffy)* Okay, Panda, I'll get you some food. Here are some bamboo shoots.
Therapist:	Gee, Fluffy, you are taking care of everyone. And who takes care of you?
Kate:	*(As Fluffy)* My friends. And I take care of myself.

DESCRIPTIVE ANALYSIS OF THE PLAY ACTIVITY

Once again, as in previous play activity, Kate used fantasy play as a vehicle for expressing her wishes. She initiated the play activity by talking with the stuffed animals; both therapist and Kate facilitate the play activity by fostering a continuous, ongoing dialogue between the characters. There was no inhibition of this lively conversation by either therapist or child. The entire play activity segment took place within the microsphere, the realm of toy animals.

Kate began the play by offering the therapist a sweet. Her offer was accepted once but not overextended to repeated feedings. Kate was turning passive into active by becoming the one who feeds, thereby vicariously enjoying the act of being fed. The roles were then switched as the therapist fed Mr. Bunny (Kate), using markers as symbolic food. Therapist and child talked about self-regulation as Mr. Bunny (Kate) responded that he hadn't eaten in a while because he "wasn't hungry." Kate also introduced the concept of not eating too much of a good thing in response to the therapist's suggestion of a very avaricious appetite. Kate responded (this time as Fluffy) about the risks of running out of the best supplies and therefore settling for something less as a regular diet (sardines in lieu of caviar). Also new in this segment was the concept of friends who nurtured and fed, as well as mother (Mommy Bunny). Kate ended the play activity segment with satiation. As a climax to the play interaction she informed the therapist (as Fluffy) that she not only received care from and gave care to others but (the caveat) could also take care of herself.

STRUCTURAL ANALYSIS OF THE PLAY ACTIVITY

Affective Components

The overall hedonic tone in this play activity segment was obvious pleasure. The spectrum of affects expressed was medium, including curiosity, pleasure, concern, and mild passive aggression (the Mommy Bunny who ignores Mr. Bunny). The transition between affective states of hunger and satiation was always smooth; regulation and modulation of feelings was flexible. Expression of feelings was usually appropriate to content, one exception being the absence of directed aggression against the negligent Mommy Bunny. Feelings expressed by Kate toward her therapist and by the therapist toward Kate were consistently positive.

Cognitive Components

Considerable complex role-play was observed in this play activity segment as Kate directed the play and became the central character for several interacting parts (Mr. Bunny, Mommy Bunny, and Fluffy, interacting with Panda and Mr. Bunny who were played by the therapist). There was also considerable evidence of dyadic role-play, particularly between Mr. Bunny and Fluffy. One instance of voluntary role transformation occurred, when the therapist and Kate switched roles. Kate became Fluffy (the maternal role) having started out as Mr. Bunny, and Mr. Bunny (the hungry one) was then played by the therapist. Kate then also became the Mommy Bunny, thereby extending her maternal, nurturing role. Representation of objects remained consistently the same. There were two occasions of change in the use of an object, where one object was used for another (crayons for carrots at the suggestion of the therapist, and a pillow for Mommy Bunny at Kate's suggestion), both examples of symbolic substitution. Throughout this play activity segment the style of representation of persons and objects was fantasy.

Narrative Components

Kate's play was all about caregiving and feeding. The characters included a family, parents and children, placing relationships portrayed within the play narrative at the oedipal level. Relationships portrayed within the narrative were both dependent and autonomous. The language used by both the therapist and Kate included talking within the metaphor, verbalization of multiple roles, and Kate's imitation of some animal sounds.

Developmental Components

Kate's play was somewhat immature for her chronological age. The gender identity of her play activity was predominantly feminine, dealing with caregiving and feeding. The oral phase was predominant in the play (caregiving and food), with some minimal evidence of latency characteristics (emphasis on autonomy and peer group). There was moderate evidence for practicing issues (being the nurturing one) and minimal evidence of object constancy issues (availability of mother). In the interactions between Kate and her therapist there was considerable evidence of reciprocity and cooperation.

FUNCTIONAL ANALYSIS OF THE PLAY ACTIVITY

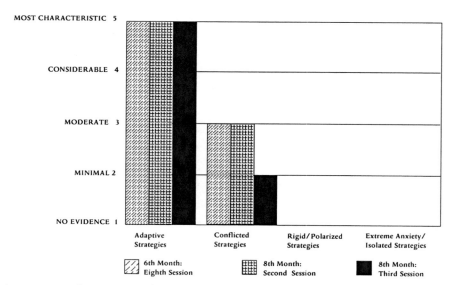

Figure 2.2 Kate's Coping–Defensive Strategies in the Course of Treatment

Play strategies observed in this last vignette were most characteristically adaptive. This play activity segment had several significant features. First, it was preceded by a non-play segment (an offer of candy to the therapist), and the theme of the non-play segment was then repeated in the play activity segment, namely feeding and the support to one's autonomy given by friends. This almost isomorphic duplication between non-play and play activity had been noted in the prior session with the creation of the Land of the Unwanted which contained objects identical with those of the playroom. This symbolic elaboration of duplication (making a duplicate of the experience) is the hallmark of *sublimation*. Using sublimation the child creates a meaningful metaphor for self-expression. Metaphor serves as a vehicle for subjective duplication. Kate's emphasis on peer relationships illustrates the use of *affiliation* and *identification*. Sharing of supplies reflects the use of *anticipation*, *altruism*, and *problem-solving*.

Second, the content of this play activity segment dealt with self-regulation and the acceptance of limits. Kate did not permit Fluffy an abundance of caviar, as supplies would run out. Kate's concept of object constancy (separation–individuation phase) seemed to be connected to an appropriate allotment of supplies. As Mommy Bunny, Kate was firm in her resolve to be available whenever needed. The regression that did occur in the play was certainly in the service of exploring her new capacities for constancy and friendship. In the first instance, she could be depended upon; in the second instance, she could depend upon others.

There was minimal evidence of conflictual strategies in this play activity segment, specifically the just-mentioned *regression* in the service of expressing early needs for nurturing and *projection* of early wishes onto the toy animals. There was no evidence of rigid/polarized strategies or extreme anxiety/isolated strategies in this play activity segment.

Kate's representation of emotional constancy and supportive friendships in her play activity reflected her growing competence to care for herself in the everyday world and to enter peer relationships without fearing rejection. This case illustrated a child's capacity to use love and warmth within the transference relationship adaptively as a secure base from which to build solid social relationships.

The next chapter will highlight the play activity of conflicted players. These children use play strategies to portray a struggle between opposing tendencies originating from within themselves or from the surroundings in which they live. These struggles create the tensions that find expression through the child's play activity.

CHAPTER 3

The Conflicted Player

The conflicted player is playing out issues he cannot resolve. These are issues of great concern to the child, issues that alternately fascinate him, trouble him, and intrigue him and that continually preoccupy him. They may include power struggles, stories that repeat and never end, desires that are unattainable, and dangers that intrigue yet can potentially devour and destroy. The conflicted player also manifests play activity strategies characteristic of the other play clusters, including adaptive strategies, but observing the conflicted player one gets the predominant impression of play activity reflecting opposing tendencies, rather than a smooth flow of creativity. The disjuncture or opposition may occur within the narrative, within interaction with the therapist, within or between the dimensions of play structure, or within the capacity of the child to sustain play activity segments. The therapist engages the child in play activity around these conflicts and becomes a participant in the child's emotional world.

Anna Freud (1963) described the case of a six-year-old child suffering from a compulsion neurosis. The child explains to Freud why she comes to see her: "I have a devil in me. Can it be taken out?" The conflict for her is between her wishes to be dirty, selfish, bad, and disgusting and her need to conform to her parents' rigid expectations of good behavior. Gradually the devil becomes known and accepted, with a reduction in associated tensions. The child uses daydreams to give voice to the feelings of being rejected and unwanted. With Freud as advisor to both child and parents, the symptoms diminish. For this group of conflicted patients, the child's wishes clash with cultural demands, resulting in inhibition of the forbidden wishes and associated symptomatology.

More recently, Edward Corrigan and Pearl-Ellen Gordon (1995) have described a different group of child patients who present with symptomatology resulting from conflict. For these child patients, the mind has become their source of security following a breakdown of early parent–child relationship. One such child is Sabrina, an eight-year-old girl who announces, much to her mother's upset, that she is not going to attend a birthday party. It is the birthday of one of her best friends, but she has lost the invitation, so she cannot go. She stubbornly insists on her decision, despite the therapist's pointing out that others are not punishing her; it is she who is tenaciously punishing herself. She replies, "Exactly right. Now you know why I can't go!" No alien introject, no devil is punishing her; rather her own rigid sense of right and wrong is keeping her from pleasure. Kerry Kelly (1970) described 5-year-old Emma, similarly precocious, who while playing at being a baby begins to crawl down the stairs very quickly. Her analyst warns, "Be careful, babies need help sometimes." Emma answers, "But it is not always there, so I manage by myself." Managing "by themselves" results in premature closure regarding moral issues; the child becomes his own parent.

These are children in conflict with their bodily and emotional needs, who have received inadequate parental regulation and care. In an attempt to adapt to this poverty of care, they come to rely very early upon the competence of their own minds. In place of loving and protective care is a precocious self-reliance on their "thinking heads" and intellectual prowess. These precocious children are exemplary of today's conflicted players. Corrigan and Gordon quote six-year-old Lilly playing a multitalented Cinderella who can do everything and anything, saying "I was born sixteen. I never had diapers, never had a bottle, no pacifier, no thumb, no baby food."

Conflicted Strategies Used By the Child at Play

The manual of the Children's Play Therapy Instrument (Kernberg, Chazan, & Normandin 1997) defines thirteen conflicted strategies that can be observed while a child is playing. These separate strategies are conceptualized as belonging to a larger cluster of conflicted play behaviors.

Intellectualization

The play activity deals with the emotional implications of the play in a neutral, factual, objective way.

"I am changing my experience into one of thoughts."

Rationalization

The child explains the play activity to the therapist using acceptable but false reasons.

"I will give myself a different reason to avoid worry."

Isolation

In the play activity ideas are separated from their threatening affects. The result is often an apparent indifference.

"I can think about it and not feel it."

Doing and Undoing

The play activity is carried out and then reversed or neutralized. There is an underlying representation of equal, opposing wishes. The cyclical quality of these play events may cause them to appear magical.

"I am placing it and then taking it away."

Negation

The child dismisses the value, meaning, or significance of the threatening feeling or behavior observed in the play activity.

"I know it could be great, but I don't care."

Reaction Formation

A warded-off idea and feeling are replaced by an expression of its opposite. Reaction formation keeps the painful idea and affect in mind; only the value is reversed.

"I will experience only the pleasant part of what happened."

Repression

The child successfully plays out a theme of which he is unaware. (The inference is made by the observer.) Repression is inferred when there is pleasurable play.

"I'm not looking. I'm not seeing and I am not aware of it."

Projection

Qualities, feelings, wishes, and thoughts of a person or object representation that the child refuses to recognize in himself or in one of the play characters are expelled and located in another person or thing.

"I am putting this outside of me into someone/something else."

Introjection

One character in the play activity transposes objects and their inherent qualities from the outside to inside his own self. The emphasis is on being the recipient of the interaction.

"I am swallowing, taking this into myself."

Regression

The child or one of the characters in the play activity reverts to modes of activity and expression characteristic of a younger child.

"I am going backwards in time."

Somatization

The child or one of the characters in the play activity is preoccupied with physical symptoms.

"My body is speaking for me."

Turning Aggression Against the Self

An unacceptable impulse is redirected by the child or one of the play characters against himself, often to protect someone else from being hurt.

"I am hitting myself."

Avoidance

The child turns away from a feared object or character; the avoidance may be only fleeting or momentary. The child has experienced the feared object or person as a threat to his functioning and withdraws from the situation in a phobic way.

"I turn away from the danger and won't even notice it."

Clinical Case: George, the Mad Scientist, and the Camera

George, five years and eleven months old, was referred to the outpatient clinic because of suicidal behavior that followed an episode when he took an inexpensive toy from a store without his mother's knowledge. When they arrived home and she discovered what he had done, his mother reprimanded him sternly, insisting they return to the store so he could confess his misdeed to the storeowner. During this discussion, George became very distraught, suddenly ran into the kitchen, grabbed a knife, and held it to his chest, threatening to stab himself. The following week George was extremely dysphoric and commented several times that his parents did not need him and he would be better off dead.

George's parents described him as a precocious, intellectually curious child, who seemed to have no emotional problems prior to the stealing. He could be defiant at home, particularly when it came time to clean up his toys or when he was expected to cooperate with efforts to get out of the house to be on time for appointments. He resorted to temper tantrums when frustrated by limits. In kindergarten, he was doing well academically and socially. The entire episode was still very shocking to them, as they recalled how violently George reacted in the days after he had stolen the toy.

Family history revealed that George's father was employed by the armed services at the time of his birth; the family was stationed outside of the United States. George's mother was alone with him a good deal during his first year of life. His infancy was marked by severe colic. The family had no outside supports to assist with child care, and his mother reported being overwhelmed by the baby's crying and her own inability to soothe him. She would sometimes close herself in the bathroom for hours to shut out the sound of the crying. During George's second year, the colic eased and the quality of their lives improved. His parents began to take delight in George's bright and inquisitive nature. When George was two years old, the family relocated to the United States. His mother was able to make social contacts beyond the family and felt less isolated. His father's new work schedule allowed him to spend more time with his family, and father and son spent enjoyable hours together. His father remembered that his favorite activity was reading scientific books to George.

When George was four years old, his younger sister was born. He was jealous of the new arrival and aggressive toward her. Shortly after her birth, the family moved again, this time to a large urban center. George had made close friends, and it was difficult for him to say good-bye. His parents noticed more oppositional behavior at this time. They attributed it to personality factors and sibling rivalry. Parent–child tension sometimes became marked during confrontations. The parents seemed to add to George's provocativeness, rather than to provide him with calm and comfort. His mother described an incident on a snowy day when George was thwarting their efforts to return home. She was feeling pressured by the demands of her schedule. At one point, he leaned over to scoop up some snow, and she, feeling exasperated, pushed him over with her foot, so that he landed head first in the snow. Mother and father laughed as she shared her fantasy of rubbing his face in the cold snow, as she watched him lying there.

Malaise, tension, and suppressed parental hostility were palpable at George's first interview, when his mother was present. George denied any suicidal ideation and volunteered to describe the stealing incident. He said he was afraid he would have to go to jail for what he did. He glanced uncomfortably at his mother at this juncture, referencing her reaction. Then he buried his head in her lap. With the therapist's support, George's mother was able to stroke his hair and reassure him that no further punishment was needed.

In the following pages, therapy sessions from the beginning, middle, and end of George's treatment are excerpted and analyzed to highlight both verbal and nonverbal aspects of the play and the unfolding process of treatment.

SEGMENTATION OF THREE THERAPY SESSIONS

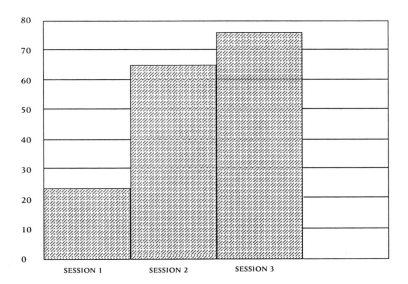

Figure 3.1 Percentage of Time in Play in the Course of George's Treatment

Since George presented as an inhibited, intellectualized, precocious child, it was anticipated that he would resist free, spontaneous play. Because of an inability to sustain play activity, early therapy sessions were expected to have individual play segments of short duration, with the child going in and out of play activity frequently. The proportion of total time spent in play during the session was expected to be low, and the time spent in non-play to be high. It was anticipated that as treatment progressed, play activity segments would increase in duration and that sessions would flow more smoothly, with fewer moves in and out of play and more time spent in play activity.

All the expectations based on George's presentation at the beginning of therapy were fulfilled. As therapy progressed, play activity segments accounted for increasing amounts of the time in his sessions, and play activity segments became longer, with fewer shifts in and out of play activity. By the third session described, from the ending phase of treatment, play activity occupied 74 percent of the session (see Figure 3.1), a clear shift from George's predominant choice of non-play activities at the beginning of treatment.

Excerpt From a Session at the Beginning of Treatment

George begins to build a tower out of markers. With eyes averted and turning partly away from the therapist, he says in an earnest voice, "You know what?" He describes how his grandma had a precious antique bureau that had belonged to his father and now belongs to him. Talking in a serious manner, he continues to connect markers together. As he describes how they had to throw out some toys to make space for the furniture, he disconnects one of the markers and begins to draw.

Therapist:	Do you miss those toys?
George:	One tiny thing, a clock. I threw it at my mom and it broke. I didn't want to clean up my room.
Therapist:	What will your parents do with the toys?
George:	They will throw them in the garbage. They *(the toys)* are like my friends. *(Looks sad, begins to draw)* I'm making a real weird animal. See—it's a flying animal and it can slide. *(Demonstrates sliding movement)*
Therapist:	Is this an animal you have seen before?
George:	I made it up. It's on my planet—Za!
Therapist:	Who lives on this planet?
George:	I used to. Of course *(goes back to connecting markers and constructing a large tower)*, the planet blew up. But I got into a spaceship. It was a heavy-duty spaceship. I blasted it. *(Uses connected markers as a space ship)*
Therapist:	You got out in time. Is the planet still there?
George:	No. *(Scatters markers all around)* It exploded.

DESCRIPTIVE ANALYSIS OF THE PLAY ACTIVITY

George began his play activity by building a tower of markers. Then he took one of the markers and began to draw. His drawing depicted a weird animal who lived on a planet from which, George tells us, the animal escaped before the planet exploded. A sense of agency as well as destructive force was communicated through his accompanying actions. Although George's words told a story, his feelings were not fully contained by the words. His intense affective expression preceded his story, and through movements he conveyed a sense of what would happen next.

Precocious verbal skills, problem-solving abilities, and a strong capacity for affiliation were positive prognostic indicators for a good outcome for George's treatment. Therapeutic issues included regulating George's aggressive impulses and freeing him from his entrenched, defensive stance. George seriously rationalized his need to be rid of the thrown-out toys, but at the same time he lamented and missed his toy "friends." The desire to act grown-up and comply with his parents' expectations undermined his true feelings. He felt sad and lonely with his friends gone. Suddenly, George shared with his therapist his secret, private universe. The story ended in disaster and rescue, barely masking George's explosive feelings. Although part of himself had escaped, part of himself, the planet where he once resided, had exploded.

George told his story through the media of art activity, construction play, and fantasy. As has been noted, his verbal themes were continually augmented by nonverbal movement. Play activity took place in the macrosphere, using everyday-sized objects in the room. George initiated the play activity on his own, and both therapist and George facilitated the unfolding of the play. George ended his play story with a bang, clearly fully satisfied with what he had created.

STRUCTURAL ANALYSIS OF THE PLAY ACTIVITY

Affective Components

Although the content of George's story was intense and explosive, his overall emotional tone was sober. Emotions he expressed fell in a somewhat narrow range and included aggression, anxiety, fear, sadness, and relief. Transitions between affect states were always abrupt, but George's affective tone was usually appropriate to the content. His attitude towards the therapist was neutral; the therapist was consistently positive in his attitude towards George.

Cognitive Components

In this play activity segment George related events that had occurred on the planet Za. In narrating and describing these events as an observer, he demonstrated a capacity for complex role-play. Neither the animal he described nor the planet underwent transformation. Although the planet disappeared (or fragmented) and became a nonentity, it did not become something else; the characters in this story retained their stable identities until the planet was destroyed. The "weird animal" was definitely a fantasy, as was the planet Za. Although magical, George's characters were not bizarre.

Narrative Components

In this story George was both the "One Who Was Caught" and the "One Who Leaves" (in a hurry). George associated themes of construction (the markers) with destruction (the planet) and escape (his own). Connecting these three themes was the terrifying underlying relationship described metaphorically in the story as annihilation by a diffuse force. George was very verbal. His use of metaphor resulted in his using language in two ways: talking during the play describing the play and talking during the play about something other than the play (his associations). Language used by the therapist during the play was mostly to inquire about ongoing events (description) and to inquire about the play (making connections between events and gaining clarifications about events).

Developmental Components

George's play was appropriate for his developmental level. There was no dominance of gender expressed in the play. The "real weird animal" was clearly different from others and reflected George's concern in perceiving himself as different from others on the planet, a differentiation issue. A practicing issue was observed in George's attempts at successfully portraying the different creature and blasting away from the exploding planet. George's blast-off on the space rocket was definitely a phallic expression of destructive separation. This forceful move outward and away from the home that could no longer protect him took place within a "heavy-duty spaceship" that could assure his survival. George played both alone in the presence of the therapist and together in cooperation with the therapist. This interaction could be translated as an expression of George's developing trust in his therapist, who provided a safe sphere within which play could develop (the "heavy-duty spaceship"). This background of safety could allow George's aggression to emerge with playfulness and without fear of retaliation.

FUNCTIONAL ANALYSIS OF THE PLAY ACTIVITY

George was consistently *aware* he was playing, but he was not fully aware of the expressive role of his nonverbal actions. As he attempted to relate to the therapist through words, he also constructed a parallel connection between markers. When his planet Za exploded, the markers were thrown helter-skelter around the room. Thus, words did not fully represent George's emotional experience, and actions were needed to expand on the emotional impact of the planet's fate. In this verbal and precocious child, early conflicts remained around the control and expression of aggression. These early conflicts needed to be "played out" in activity *(regression)*. In the service of playing, George relied heavily upon a relationship with the therapist *(affiliation)* and his creative imagination to design alternative fantasy solutions to his real-life dilemma *(problem-solving)*.

The verbal narrative unfolded in counterpoint to nonverbal play activity, one complemented the other. George gave a full, continuous verbal account of the fantasy and real-life events over which he had no control, such as the throwing of one tiny clock (an angry *projection* when asked to pick up his toys), or the explosion of the planet Za. Through nonverbal play activity (construction of a tower and drawing of a creature) and the abundant use of *projection*, George was able to maintain some sense of control and agency over events narrated in the dialogue. Loss of control was expressed through activity as well as fantasy, for example when the erect tower of markers toppled and scattered. The exploding planet had been his secure haven; this former protective container for the self was forcefully shattered *(aggression against the self)*. George used strategies of *avoidance* and *reaction formation* to disguise and deny these threatening impulses. Instead, our hero rescued himself by blasting away from the threat of annihilation. In order to accomplish this feat, George needed to use more potent defensive strategies, strategies characteristic of rigid/polarized players (discussed in Chapter 4) and even of extremely anxious/isolated players (discussed in Chapter 5). *Omnipotent control* and *idealization* of his own creative abilities enabled him to achieve the powers he needed. The tower of markers that had previously tumbled was transformed into a magically empowered vehicle. In scattering and disorganizing his play materials *(dispersal)* George depicted his greatest terror (disintegration of the self); separation from planet Za assured his survival. As his therapist reflected, "You got out in time."

Excerpt From a Session Midway in Treatment

Play activity began to open with nonverbal expression as George increasingly made more direct efforts to approach and interact with his therapist (note the creeping, crawling creatures). As their relationship deepened, George was often taken by surprise as unanticipated new fantasy characters appeared alongside familiar ones.

George:	*(Brings his eye to the video camera)*
Therapist:	Good shot. I can see your eye real close.
George:	*(Covers camera lens with his hand)*
Therapist:	Where did the movie go?
George:	*(Smiling, dangles fingers in front of lens)*
Therapist:	More of those creepy, crawly things…
George:	*(Brings small toys—spiders, small dinosaurs and triceratops)*
Therapist:	*(Cautions George not to touch lens of camera)*
George:	*(Brings a toy car to the camera, then shoots a toy gun at the camera. Approaching the blackboard, George appears to be in a pensive mood)* Oh! *(He draws a turtle with stripes on its back)*
Therapist:	Interesting picture. *(George goes to erase it)* Can I guess what it is? A turtle. A turtle is now in our movie.
George:	Guess. *(He takes paper, draws a picture and holds the picture next to the camera lens and moves it around)*
Therapist:	Can you say what is happening? What does it look like?
George:	Maybe a weird scientist…going into the black hole.
Therapist:	Will he come out of it?
George:	No. No one comes out of the black hole. *(He continues to draw)*
Therapist:	He would be scared, wouldn't he? Did you ever go into a black hole?
George:	No.
Therapist:	Were you ever scared it might happen?
George:	*(While drawing)* No—only—*(repeats with stutter)*, know what? There is this one constellation where there is

something really special about it. *(George places black hole on the camera)*

Therapist: Hold it back further so that we can see.

George: *(Holds up a sign that says "George," then takes a dinosaur and dangles it before the camera. He then takes a knife and wields it before the camera)*

Therapist: That's knife-wielding George, "Samurai George."

George: *(Shoots gun at camera. Next he makes a Lego plane that zooms into camera. Then he gestures making binoculars and looking intensely into the lens)*

Therapist: Hey, out there! Hello, out there!

George: *(Ends fantasy play activity by suggesting they play chess)*

Therapist and child proceed to prepare for the next game encounter. The playful interaction with the therapist via the camera lens is discontinued; the confrontation is continued in a more structured play form.

DESCRIPTIVE ANALYSIS OF THE PLAY ACTIVITY

In the play activity, George continued to adapt play materials in a creative way. He made contact with the threatening observing other (the camera) and fought against it, in an effort to ward off the threat posed by regressed and depressive feelings inherent in the image of the black hole. George's sense of self was under siege by these strong aversive feelings that he could no longer ignore.

The therapist's mirroring, empathic stance enabled George to continue his construction of a safe arena in which to explore these overwhelming feelings. The emergence of a sense of self (as a very special constellation), an active, assertive (at times scary) self, could be represented, given the supportive presence of the therapist. Many of these images were enacted through mime rather than described, an indication of George's vulnerability to *regression*. The therapist's attunement to George's nonverbal communication led to the appearance of the "mad scientist" who could receive and understand his alien messages, a clear reference to emerging scary feelings of intimacy within the transference relationship and a distant reference to his scientific father.

George's play was fantasy and used drawings *(art activity)* to gain full expression. It was initiated nonverbally by George when he engaged the camera in eye-to-eye contact. The play activity was facilitated by both therapist and child; the therapist continued his inquiries into fantasy events, and George maintained an active repartee in response. There was no evidence of inhibition in the play activity, which took place in both the realm of toys *(microsphere)* and the real world *(macrosphere)*. The ending of the play segment was initiated by George, who aggressively approached the camera (with a knife and a zooming plane) and then introduced eye-to-eye contact from a new perspective with the use of binoculars. He seemed satisfied with this fantasy play and chose to continue the therapeutic encounter in the form of a more structured game. The dyad made a transition through a period of pre-play to playing chess.

STRUCTURAL ANALYSIS OF THE PLAY ACTIVITY

Affective Components

George was having fun during this playful segment; his overall hedonic tone was pleasurable interest. The spectrum of affects was wide, from delight to fear. Although George was clearly delighted with his new escapades and discoveries (for example, the creepy crawly things), he appeared to be surprised and a bit frightened by their unexpected appearance. Feelings expressed by George included aggression, anxiety, curiosity, delight, fear, sadness, and wariness. This widening of the spectrum of feelings expressed is an indication that George's defenses are loosening as he becomes aware of feelings previously hidden and protected from awareness. As would be expected given George's heightened level of anxiety, the regulation of his feeling states was not smooth, despite the increased range of his affective responsiveness. The modulation of his feelings was somewhat rigid, and the transition between his affective states was usually abrupt. George was very connected to the unfolding of the play encounters, and his affective tone was consistently appropriate to the content of the play. The therapist's affective tone toward George was very positive; he clearly enjoyed his interactions with him. George's affective tone toward his therapist was somewhat positive but also tinged by apprehension.

Cognitive Components

In this play activity midway in treatment, George again used complex role representations to describe and direct many different characters. It was significant, however, that none of these creatures interacted with each other. Rather, they appeared before the camera, in mime and pictures, and were designated by name; no plot emerged between them. In fact, George seemed surprised by the appearance of some of his characters, such as the turtle, while he was clearly fearful of others (squirmy, crawly creatures and the large dinosaurs). The therapist attempted to elicit action between the characters. In a parallel role it was he, the brave "mad scientist" (a personification of aspects of the transference relationship), who ventured into the black hole. Then, George diverted attention from the scary black hole to the creation of a very special constellation named "George." "George" appeared in the place of former nothingness. By inference, it seemed to require the "weird scientist's" spunk and courage to explore and thereby facilitate George's act of self-discovery. In contrast to the previous play activity segment, in which survival depended upon omnipotent powers, this emergence of self occurred through the combined efforts of a partnership—the explorer and the artist.

The camera was an important participant in this dialogue, a silent partner who contained all the images projected into it. The camera did not react to aggression and was able to absorb these feelings without retaliating. George was able to interact in this way with the observing, nonverbal camera. He gained courage at the end of the play segment, approached the camera closely, and carefully peered inside the lens. The camera functioned as a benevolent other (another aspect of the transference relationship between therapist and patient), inviting curiosity and intimacy.

In this play activity toys were used predominantly for realistic purposes (for example, a gun to shoot) and did not transform. Under George's control, however, the black hole did undergo change. It was not transformed totally but receded and became a background for the emergence of a special constellation named "George." As noted above, many of the characters were represented through actions and the use of mime. The characters described were mostly real, but some characters also presented with a blend of realistic and fantasy features (for example, the "weird scientist" and the turtle, which had stripes on its back).

Narrative Components

George's play included diverse topics including doctor, natural forces, fighting, attacking, the "One Who Might Be Caught," and the "One Who Is Resurrected." The diverse topics cue us in to the nature of the conflict that George experienced as a need to fight off powerful forces that might lead to his destruction. This inclusion of possibility is a departure from the absolute power of certainty. George was depending upon the resources, energy, and support of his doctor to become the "One Who Is Reborn." The idealization and grandiose scale of this conflict suggested the threat of underlying feelings of helplessness. The theme of the play activity, a struggle between life and death, reflected the ultimate terms in which George understood his conflict. Relationships within the play narrative were pervasively influenced by the threat of destruction emanating from identifiable sources (the black hole, killer, "Samurai George").

George's use of language was limited in this play activity segment to talking during the play to describe the play. The therapist's use of language was quantitatively more abundant and diverse. He used language to describe the play, to speak within the metaphor of the play, and to talk about the meaning of the play.

Developmental Components

In this play segment George's play was developmentally appropriate for his chronological age. The aggressive, assertive actions (fighting, shooting) evident in the play are associated in our culture with predominantly phallic, masculine activities. In this play, George was focused upon practicing his strengths, going back for new weapons and then returning to the struggle. His sadistic assertions and subsequent fearful retreats to security suggested issues dominant during the rapprochement subphase of separation–individuation. George's bravado also suggested the expression of some concern about prowess (practicing subphase). In interaction with his therapist, George combined cooperative play with a few moments of retreat to solitary (aware) play.

FUNCTIONAL ANALYSIS OF THE PLAY ACTIVITY

In this session, the tendency to disperse and scatter toy objects (*dispersal*) as a response to stress was markedly absent. Instead of disorganization, attack by an identifiable aggressor and the need for protection became the focus of play activity. Using these strategies George was able to demonstrate an emergent capacity for trust in his therapist. The growing resilience of their relationship *(affiliation, identification)* was reflected in the considerable use of adaptive coping strategies. George was able to use play materials creatively and began to appreciate his therapist's sense of *humor* and to use humor himself (for example, in exaggerated gestures, the "weird scientist"). The humor was based on attunement to his own anxieties, as well as attunement to how these anxieties appeared from the perspective of a different "lens" (diminished and incongruous). Humor acted to counteract and defuse the constrictions imposed upon his play by fearfulness. Feeling less constrained, George was freer to experiment with modifications in his play and even to experiment with closeness, as he peered into the eye of the beholding camera. Finally, George demonstrated the use of positive expectation *(anticipation)* when he began to respond to the therapist's queries as to what might happen next in the emerging narrative.

Coping strategies indicating the presence of conflict between wishes and actions, between conscious thoughts and thoughts of which he was not aware, were also a strong focus in the play. George made considerable use of *projection* to give voice to his ideas through the medium of play characters. *Regression* was observed in his advances to the camera's lens, conveying his hunger for early visual attunement and recognition.

George used *avoidance* in an attempt to regulate his level of arousal when he covered the lens with his hand (akin to playing peek-a-boo with the camera lens) and the therapist inquired, "Where did the movie go?" There was clear conflict over giving expression to these early tactile (creepy, crawling things) and visual longings for contact. George countered by using *intellectualization* to transform these play interactions into scientific forays. His efforts to shoot and attack the camera were *reaction formations* against these threatening needs for closeness. Being assertive and threatening himself seemed to reassure George, and he was then able to reconnoiter the camera once again (from a distance, using binoculars). What George was searching for through his actions was the best distance (perspective) from which to view and connect with this desired/threatening object.

George's capacity for *identification with the aggressor* served him well in this play activity. Being strong and taking the offensive, George could relinquish almost completely his efforts to have omnipotent control. His presentation as strong and phallic warded off his feelings of being tiny and unprotected. These polarized defensive strategies were becoming less rigidly organized as George allowed himself to play about the flow and regulation of his feelings. One reminder of George's loneliness and isolation occurred in the use of *dedifferentiation* to represent the black hole. In the emptiness of the black hole the dread of nonrecognition was fully represented. In the nothingness of blackness, all parts were the same and everything was reduced to nothing. In using this representation George was alluding to early experiences of disconnection from caregivers and the persistence of despair and depression in his emotional life. There was poignancy in the potential for rebirth that occurred once his worst fears had been represented, reflected upon, and shared. It was, after all, the "weird (anxiety-arousing/strange/fascinating) scientist" (intellectual) who had the courage to venture forth and made the discovery of a new constellation called "George."

Excerpt From a Session During Ending Phase of Treatment

George initiates a storytelling game with the therapist, and they begin to select picture cards. At first George is subdued, then he laughs mischievously and joins in sorting paper characters.

George:	This is the doctor who takes them home and cooks them for dinner!
Therapist:	Mean doctor!
George:	Not a doctor, a scientist. *(He tosses the doctor figure into the air)* Everyone gets cooked for dinner *(George throws the characters in the air)* Ga-ga. This is a doctor, too *(chooses character)*. They fight!
Therapist:	Looks like the people are very angry at each other. Is that the end of the story?

George:	*(Challenging)* Don't I get a chip *(reward for story)*? *(Stands on his head)*
Therapist:	What does this mean?
George:	Not go to the doctor. Not the mad scientist doctor.
Therapist:	Doctors can't be trusted.

(Long silence. George continues to sort out the characters, therapist's gaze is averted. While grimacing mischievously, George grabs several chips)

George:	I win. Nine to ten. I tricked you. *(Laughs)*
Therapist:	There's Mr Tricky. *(George laughs)* Mr Tricky is so rich.

(Therapist looks away)

George:	*(Steals chips)*
Therapist:	Where are the chips? Where did they go?
George:	I ate them. *(He is on his knees and he falls forward onto the floor with the upper part of his body curled in fetal position)*
Therapist:	Where are the chips?
George:	*(Giggles, bends over in laughter. Raises himself up on his knees and falls forward again)*
Therapist:	You ate my chips!
George:	*(Laughs. Falls forward. Raises self up on haunches and points)* There's a tree behind you!
Therapist:	*(Turns to look)*
George:	*(Takes more chips and doubles over in laughter)* Look out the window!
Therapist:	I'm afraid to look! *(Turns to look)*
George:	*(Giggles. Steals)*
Therapist:	What did you do?
George:	I didn't take anything. *(Long giggles. Distracts therapist and steals)* I tricked you again! Want to play a game? Want to see how they clean up at school? *(George messes all the pieces)* "Clean Up."

Therapist:	What does the teacher say?
George:	*(George screams in laughter with jeering tone. He continues to make a mess)*
Therapist:	Is that when the baby comes out?
George:	Where's the baby? There's no baby. I'm not a baby. I'm a big boy.
Therapist:	We all have a baby side.
George:	I don't have a baby side.
Therapist:	Sure, we all have a baby side. I see your baby side. Show the camera your baby side.
George:	*(George turns towards the camera, sucking thumb, while smiling. The infant expression transforms into a cruel monster face. The monster has a threatening, angry expression, with open mouth and bared teeth. George turns to therapist and laughs with his head back. George turns to face the camera again with exaggerated monster face. He turns back again to the therapist and raises his arms in a menacing gesture. With this expression he returns to face the camera and then back to the therapist)*
Therapist:	Oh, that's the monster side. Show the camera your angry side.
George:	*(Angry grimace to camera)*
Therapist:	What is that side?
George:	My big-big tooth side. *(Giggles and then attacks therapist, all the while giggling)* Show me your scary face!
Therapist:	*(Does his imitation of George)*
George:	*(Jumps away and onto couch, hiding his head in the pillows, immersed in giggles)*
Therapist:	Is it scary?
George:	Show me again! *(Shrieks in laughter, jumps on couch, burrowing his head)*

The therapist suggests they pick up the pieces of the game. George goes to the shelf and takes out a game of checkers. He picks up a few characters and quickly sets up the board. The board game follows, with George following the rules. First the therapist is winning; the tables are turned when George executes a double jump. The therapist playfully tries to distract George and steal some of his pieces back. They engage in a repeat of the stealing game, this time with the therapist as culprit. The therapist agrees to stop his stealing and the game of checkers continues uneventfully for another ten minutes, with George eventually winning. George helps to put the board game away and inquires if he can come to see the therapist for another year. The therapist says he will need to discuss his request with his parents, however, they still have eight planned sessions before they end. George begins to playfully box with the therapist. The therapist allows George to play at fighting him. He comments that George seems upset and angry at the thought of ending. Upon leaving they agree to talk more about ending next time they meet.

DESCRIPTIVE ANALYSIS OF THE PLAY ACTIVITY

In this session, direct interaction appeared between George and his therapist. Forbidden impulses were enacted through pantomime, along with associated affects. High-pitched, tremulous, intense laughter accompanied provocative, assertive "in your face" movements. These provocations were balanced by slow, stealthy movements, attempting to hide secretive, *forbidden* activities. Playful falling from sight (collapsing) and hidden movements shielded the protagonists (therapist and child) from dangerous angry and messy wishes. The challenge to the observer was to untangle George and his therapist from among the quickly transforming roles.

George initiated the fantasy play by selecting the picture cards for a game. Both therapist and child participated actively in the game, facilitating direct interactions and confrontation with George's infantile feelings. There was no evidence of inhibition of play activity by either therapist or child. The playing gained momentum and was ended by the therapist because the session was ending. George agreed to end the play; he reluctantly made the transition to non-play as he joined in cleaning up and expressed the desire to extend the number of planned therapy sessions. The play took place entirely within the realm of everyday surroundings *(macrosphere)*; there were no small toys used in the play *(microsphere)*.

STRUCTURAL ANALYSIS OF THE PLAY ACTIVITY

Affective Components

George's affective response to playfulness changed dramatically during the course of treatment. This last play activity segment was obviously pleasurable for George. He felt very positive feelings for his therapist; his therapist felt very positive feelings for him. George felt comfortable in expressing a wide spectrum of feelings, including aggression, anger, anxiety, curiosity, fear, pleasure, wariness, and feigned indifference. George was flexible in his modulation of feelings. The transitions between affective states (fear to fun to anger) fluctuated: at times they were smooth and at other times they were abrupt. This more fluent, fluid affective responsiveness was one of the markers of George's therapeutic progress.

Cognitive Components

In this play activity segment George relinquished his controlling style and played interactively with his therapist. The play activity was predominantly dyadic role-play, with the therapist and George as partners. Minimal evidence of complex role-play occurred at the beginning of the session, when George directed the play describing themes of cannibalism between characters. George's play definitely became more spontaneous and less intellectualized. The roles of therapist and George underwent voluntary transformations as they reversed "cat and mouse" positions. Play activity ended with the revelation of two important characters, the needy baby and the threatening monster. These two representations gave expression to George's underlying conflict in a graphic and dramatic manner. The therapist was not threatened by the outburst of aggression and encouraged George to share these feelings with the camera. George complied and then asked the therapist to do his scary face. The therapist's imitation of George's expression triggered squeals of delight as George recognized this replication of his expression. In this session it was the players, the people, that changed roles, while play objects did not transform. Similarly, play objects were portrayed realistically (for example, the game chips), while the play characters (doctor, robber) were fantasy.

Narrative Components

The play narrative was rich, detailed, and revealing. The doctor–scientist was a combination of barely concealed paternal traits. This was the adult man who could not be trusted. Out of his greediness the mean doctor took his patients home and cooked them for dinner. George's wishes to go home with his doctor were warded off by the unacceptable and scary thought that he might be devoured. Also being expressed (although projected onto the doctor) were George's own greediness and wishes to devour the doctor. This was the killing aspect of the mean doctor and of George himself. His mischievous laughter was a clue to his recognition of aspects of himself as projected into the other. The story ended in chaos as all the characters got mixed up and fought with each other.

The question of rules and boundaries was explored further as George's hunger (he wanted to eat the chips) led him to try to trick his therapist by stealing and hiding the chips. Again and again the thief appeared to divert his victim's attention and trick him. The character of the thief represented George's rebellion against compliance with the demands of an untrustworthy (yet desired) doctor/scientist (father) who left him hungry, greedy, and without provisions. This blended character combined attributes of caregiving, "weirdness," and intellectual curiosity. The baby/monster was another combination character blending two conflicting aspects of George. This unfulfilled infantile neediness and resultant aggression appeared in combination to undermine socialization. "Trickiness" was a strategy targeted to deal with these unresolved feelings, as nothing could be relinquished to the untrustworthy caregiver. George successfully turned passive into active by playing at being the thief who took his revenge against the greedy, mean adult. Messiness and breaking the rules assured the baby/monster of victory. In this way the baby/monster would always win and triumph over competition.

Within the play narrative relationships depicted included dependence (patient on doctor, child on parent), malevolent control (doctor of patient, parent of child), and destruction by an identifiable agent (the rage of the parent, the retaliation of the child). George used language minimally in his play, but he verbalized in many different ways. He used babbling ("Ga-ga") when he enacted the role of baby, and he used language to describe the play and to talk about the meaning of the play (mainly to negate the therapist's interpretations). In contrast, the therapist made considerable use of language to verbalize multiple roles, to talk about the meaning of the play, and to a lesser extent to describe the play.

Developmental Components

The developmental level of the play activity ran the gamut from very immature to age appropriate. Gender roles observed in the play activity were both masculine (scientist, doctor) and feminine (baby, teacher); there was no predominance in gender role expression. Separation–individuation phases represented in the play also ran the gamut from differentiation ("How am I different from you?") to practicing (playing at trickery) to rapprochement issues ("good versus bad"). Unique to this session was the direct interaction between the players and George's increased variability and flexibility in social response. The social level of the play (interaction with the therapist) was completely reciprocal.

FUNCTIONAL ANALYSIS OF THE PLAY ACTIVITY

The safe confines of therapy enabled George to express and explore early wishes and needs without fearing retaliation or loss of relationship (*affiliation*). Thus, in an apparent paradox, his growing self-efficacy was reflected in a growing playful tolerance for the unacceptable and an expression of the charming and spontaneous aspects of his infantile self. *Regression* when it occurred was in the service of the ego. This backward glance enabled George to explore his earliest feelings of oral craving for supplies and anal messiness. Growing up, George had prematurely surrendered these basic needs to rules imposed by others and the dictates of intellect.

Adaptive strategies used by George included considerable use of *humor, anticipation, sublimation*, and *identification*. By establishing a connection between the robber and the doctor, the constellation and the black hole, the observing camera and all of his creatures, George gained the capacity to form cross-identifications. Only by communicating with the therapist using nonverbal signs and symbols could George reveal the hidden, feared part of himself. Once these intense longings were revealed and shared in playful activity, George felt recognized and understood by himself and his therapist.

Indications of conflict were still center stage at this point in the treatment. George's laughter was tinged at times by mania, a kind of overarousal and excitement. This excited laughter was an example of *reaction formation*, when George made scary things appear funny so that his intense feelings could be tolerated. For example, the therapist did his imitation of George's "big tooth" side, and George jumped away, hiding his head in the pillows. When the therapist inquired "Is it scary?" George shrieked "Show me again!" as he jumped on the couch burrowing his head in the pillows. At this point in his play, George was right on the cusp between play and terror. It is the therapist–patient relationship that tipped the balance to the side of safety and play. *Doing and undoing* was another strategy used in the play to forestall fear. For example, George would negate his baby side in interaction with the therapist and then reveal it to the camera. Other conflictual strategies observed included the continued use of considerable *projection* and *regression*.

Rigid/polarized play strategies were not present in this play activity segment. *Dispersal*, an extreme anxiety/isolated defense, occurred minimally at a point of disorganization. In George's story, the adult doctor took all the characters home and ate them for dinner. This oral cannibalism was accompanied by a regressive "Ga-ga" from George, and the characters got thrown into the air. It was followed by George's statement that he did not want to go to the doctor, not the "mad scientist" doctor. The therapist responded, "Doctors can't be trusted." A long silence followed. The next play events led to George's acting out his tricks and stealing reward chips. Like the doctor who could not be trusted, George consumed his prey (played at eating the chips).

George's CPTI Profile Over Eight Months of Treatment

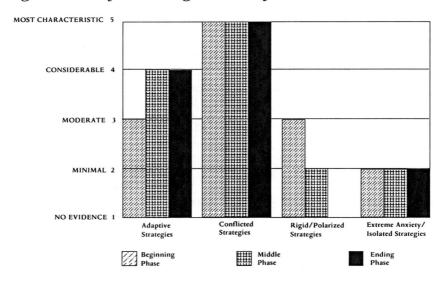

Figure 3.2 George's Coping–Defensive Strategies in the Course of Treatment

In a review of the shifts in George's coping/defensive strategies over the course of treatment, the largest change is seen in the elimination of observations in Cluster 3 (Rigid/Polarized strategies). Cluster 2 (Conflicted strategies) remained most characteristic throughout the treatment, coexisting at the end of treatment with increased Cluster 1 (Adaptive) strategies. Cluster 4 (Extreme Anxiety/Isolated) defenses remained minimally present throughout. What can we learn from the progression of coping/defensive strategies observed in play activity during this brief (eight-month) therapeutic intervention? George continued to confront early infantile needs and at moments to lose control. These ideas and wishes became counterbalanced, however, so they appeared in more adaptive, sublimated, playful ways. The feelings of helplessness could be shared as frustrations at the end of a session; the black hole no longer beckoned as an intimidating, lonely place. Indeed, George encountered a new best friend, an expanded constellation of feelings he could now identify as his own. The CPTI profile documents this shift away from impulsivity to addressing conflicts in a more metaphorical way capable of modulation and symbolic expression (see Figure 3.2).

Analyzing George's play activity with the CPTI, we observed how George used *identifications* and cross-identifications to compensate for deficits in parental attunement and referencing in early childhood. George's black hole represented the absence of an available attachment figure. Following the venturing of the "scientist" into the hole, George gave birth to his own self. This emergence of self suggested George's yearning for a male identification figure, his disillusionment with mother, and his need to depend on his own independent creative resources.

The roles enacted sequentially included the "mean doctor" who can't be trusted, the "robber" who steals, and the cruel "monster–baby." George played at being the monster–baby and asked the therapist to enact the same role. As he initiated cross-identification, we recalled D. W. Winnicott's (1971) description of "you be me and I'll be you" as the basis for the wholesome, creative aspects of introjective/projective processes. George challenged his therapist to put himself in his place. George was testing: Did the therapist have a basic understanding of others? More specifically, did he have a sense of what it felt like to be George, especially the demanding, regressive, troublesome George? Only if the therapist could play his role (and he did, to George's delight) could George grasp the experience that someone else could understand what he felt. Only then could he proceed to consolidate the capacity to understand intuitively the commonalties of experience, the capacity to see himself in others and others in himself.

As described by Elsa First (1994), by using cross-identifications George experienced first-hand how his experience of being George could become more fluid and imaginatively more exchangeable. It was precisely this newly expanded imaginative capacity that actively diminished the effects of rigid/polarized defenses in his play activity. George's capacity to observe himself (his observing ego) was reflected in his consistent awareness of himself as a player, and in his strong directorial abilities to represent diverse roles. George could now play at having and sharing affective experiences without experiencing the fear of turning into the other person. He could more truly be himself and at the same time more truly share in the experiences of others. It was failure of this reciprocal to-and-fro understanding to develop that mired George in intellectual defenses and conflict surrounding recognition of his own human feelings.

In the last play activity segment, George played at pretending, hiding and being found. His actions resonated with peek-a-boo games ubiquitous to early childhood. Anni Bergman discussed (1999) how this mutually regulated game of hiding and being discovered can become the vehicle for a child's growing capacity for imaginative exchange. In this game, George at last felt sufficiently safe to reveal himself, secure in the knowledge of his therapist's acceptance. He experimented with hiding and transforming into another menacing character, knowing full well that each time the therapist would welcome him back into reciprocal interaction. No feeling would be too adversarial; no experience would be unacceptable.

At the close of treatment, George had fully discovered the realm of play, where everything was possible and nothing was unpardonable. George discovered this play realm in the presence of another, the therapist, who at this point was not only a presence but also a partner in pretend. Shifts in the profile of coping–defensive strategies indicated how reliance on mind alone had constricted George's overall development.

In treatment the range of strategies enacted in play activity revealed roots of conflict from earliest infancy. These markers of early turmoil remained in the experiences of *dispersal* and *dedifferentiation*, compensated in part by reliance early in treatment on *omnipotent control* and *identification with the aggressor*. As George's affect became less constricted, the flow of *identifications* opened new options for *sublimation* and modulation of the strict commands of conscience. George emerged freed of the rigid constraints that brought him to treatment.

The children in the next chapter struggle with even more sharply defined archetypes in their play. These children are more restricted in their possibilities for engagement and interaction with others through play activity. We will follow from process notes the treatment of two cases manifesting a predominance of rigid/polarized play strategies.

CHAPTER 4

The Rigid/Polarized Player

Rigid and polarized play lacks the regularity of flow, modulation, and gradual change usually characteristic of play activity. Change, when it does occur, happens suddenly. It may be marked by abrupt interruptions, which may have idiosyncratic meanings. Characterizations may be limited to stereotypes with a narrow focus and not expand to convey a range of possibilities of self-expression. The play activity may appear superficial, or alternatively the fantasy depicted may be remote and encapsulated. In these instances the player is stuck in his set patterns, losing touch with the pleasurable, unexpected moment of spontaneous interaction.

Polarized play activity is always rigid, and it is further regimented by the segregation of opposites. The child may depict sharp contrasts in an adversarial scenario, or he may depict only one side of the conflict, leaving the other perspective to the inference of the viewer. Within the transference, feelings for the therapist may fluctuate sharply and result in abrupt changes of affect and behavior.

These two types of play activity—rigid and polarized—have been grouped together because they both are characterized by restriction. These restrictions sharply diminish the integrating value of the play activity for the player. Indeed, these types of play are expressive of a gap or failure that the player experiences in coping with the stress of threatening circumstances. The severe degree of threat may lead the player to shut down or cut off from the area of disturbance. Alternatively, if the intensification of the threatening situation in the play activity becomes unbearable, the child may lose control and "act out" his impulses or interrupt the play activity and leave the room.

Rigid/Polarized Defensive Strategies Used by the Child at Play

At this point along the spectrum of coping/defensive strategies, the child's emphasis is primarily on the defensive aspects of play activity. As the child perceives a greater degree of threat, he becomes increasingly preoccupied with defense of the self from threatening thoughts, feelings, and interaction. The child's focus in play activity reflects this defensive position.

Denial

The child refuses to recognize the reality of a traumatic experience, a painful affect, or a facet of the external world.

> "I am shutting off, closing myself off from that (painful) experience. I make believe it didn't happen, or it doesn't exist."

Splitting

The child sets apart attributes of himself or the other by showing lack of concern about or denial of contradictions. The threatening attribute is not recognized as an aspect of the self or as an aspect of the other person.

> "The two contradictory aspects of 'me' or the 'other' person are separate and disconnected."

Projective Identification

Bad/aggressive parts of the self or other persons are externalized into others who are experienced as dangerous. Fear of retaliation makes the child defend himself by keeping others under control to prevent them from attacking.

> "The attribute (or experience) is outside of me. 'I' am actively holding it at arm's length so it does not return to me."

Primitive Idealization

The person or object is valued above all others because of a characteristic or characteristics that cannot be duplicated. This attribute casts a magical, powerful spell, giving power and authority to the self or the other.

"You are perfect, pure, kind, and powerful. Being with you I can be like you."

"I am perfect, pure, kind, and powerful. Being with me you can be like me."

Primitive Devaluation

The child devalues himself or the other completely. He is rejected as disgusting and abhorrent, dismissed as having no importance, and may appear sinister or threatening. The devaluation is complete and focuses on one characteristic or set of characteristics that causes the self or the other person to be unacceptable, with no redeeming features.

"You are no good."

Omnipotent Control

The child attempts to control the external world by being all-powerful and coercive, expecting to be treated in a special way.

"I must keep everyone under my control."

Identification With the Aggressor

The child identifies with the "bad person" who intrudes and aggresses upon the others. By playing the strong man, he quells his anxiety about being weak and vulnerable.

"I am big and strong and can do as I please."

Discussion of the two cases that follow will use categories from the CPTI (Kernberg, Chazan, & Normandin 1997) in summaries of sessions, based on process notes. Rather than individual session ratings, global ratings are given to phases of treatment. The phases described (beginning, middle, and ending of treatment) cover several therapeutic sessions, highlighting the types of behaviors, feelings, and activities observed in each phase. This summary adaptation of the CPTI enables the therapist to describe therapeutic progress using discrete categories to condense the course of treatment. Summary use of the parameters of play activity is particularly helpful in charting progress in treatment when observations have been recorded as process notes. Global analysis lacks the precision of videotaped observations, but it is a pragmatic clinical application of the scale when videotaping is not desired.

Clinical Case: Rebecca "The Perfect One" and the "Witch"

Encountering six-and-a-half-year-old Rebecca provided the opportunity to observe problems that become manifest when a young girl's development is seriously impinged upon by familial collusion with cultural ideals. Working with Rebecca and her family posed the following questions: Does early injury to the development of self manifest itself differently in males and females, reflecting rigid cultural stereotypes? What form is characteristic of the feminine ideal? How is that form expressed in our culture? How is it manifested in the young girl? The roots of the young girl's dilemma may originate in earliest childhood, but new challenges are presented by the oedipal period, including issues of triangulation, rivalry, and the increasingly distinctive role of her relationship to father. How can these challenges be met by the young girl, and how can they be resolved satisfactorily in order to adapt to the school-age period of latency? What role does play activity have in the transition from the "little girl" of early childhood to "big girl" of school age?

Rebecca's development had been compromised by cultural ideals and family values. The challenge to therapy was to free her from the influences inhibiting her growth and prepare her for a transition to increased autonomy. Play activity would play a major part in her recovery.

Rebecca's issues touched on some important cultural gender differences in the development of self-esteem. In our society, male self-esteem develops as assertiveness and directness. In extreme instances these characteristics develop into a macho style of bravado, an exaggerated form of male grandiosity. In the young girl self-absorption is expressed differently. It is characterized by such adjectives as "beautiful," "well-behaved," "adorable," "compliant," "subservient," "dependent." Rebecca's parents associated these attributes with their daughter as a young child.

In narcissistic pathology, early injury to the self occurs when these characteristics are rigidly organized, replicating expectations of the culture that are being transmitted through the family. The young girl's grandiosity, unlike masculine bravado, is silent; it is conforming and synchronous with parental desires. Narcissistic pathology in little girls may be seen as pathological only when these narcissistic defenses for compliance are breached; the little girl is considered to be problematic only when she is unable to fulfill the ideals expected of her. Thus, Rebecca's parents became concerned because their daughter was not living up to expectations and was becoming increasingly withdrawn. Prior to the challenges of school age, compliance provides security for young girls and often parades in silent collusion with parental and cultural expectations. When Rebecca entered school, and as she faced new and different demands for initiative, achievement, and independence, compliance posed problems for her.

On entering therapy, Rebecca was six and a half years old. She presented with an aloofness and sense of entitlement expressed in a haughty attitude. In addition to demands for attention, she was a perfectionist, hypersensitive to the evaluation of others. She presented herself as a teenager, precociously concerned with her appearance, beauty, and sexual attractiveness. There was a seductive quality to her behavior that placed her constantly at center stage. At the time of referral, Rebecca met the criteria for narcissistic personality disorder in childhood (Beren 1998).

Rebecca's parents brought her for treatment because she had become emotionally withdrawn and moody since her entrance in first grade. They perceived her problems to have begun in kindergarten, when she first exhibited a lack of motivation and took no pride in her work. Her initiative continued to deteriorate until she reached a point where she seemed to lack any sense of agency. Her mother's dominant attitude was of disappointment in her daughter. In school, Rebecca was learning at a slow rate, despite good native ability and no evidence of developmental deficits. She was extremely sensitive to shame and did not seem to understand that effort was needed for achievement. She held herself apart from expectations for her age group and demanded immediate recognition, despite her inability to perform. She seemed to be enacting the role of a star performer who had somehow lost her talent and star status but could not adapt to this changed reality.

Most puzzling to Rebecca's parents was the emergence of separation problems at age six. Initial adjustment to preschool had occurred without difficulty. Earlier socialization with peers reportedly presented no problems. Despite moodiness in kindergarten, she had separated well. This year, as her withdrawal and avoidance increased, she had become clingy and was avoiding new experiences. She was refusing play dates and resisted forming new friendships. These regressive trends were not at all consistent with Rebecca's view of herself as more a teenager than a young girl. This disparity caused her endless upset, adding to her overall experience of frustration and envy of others who did not have this problem.

Rebecca lived with her parents and younger brother, aged three and a half years, in a single-family house in an affluent suburban neighborhood. She was the product of a normal pregnancy and delivery, a happy infant who slept well and was visually alert. She was always more expressive verbally than physically active. At times she seemed to lack physical stamina and always needed her naps. She was "dainty and feminine and did not like roughhouse play." Toilet training was achieved at two and a quarter years with no difficulty. There were no serious illnesses or family losses. Rebecca was prone to upper respiratory infections and would run high fevers, which caused parental worry. Reportedly until age three years she was a happy, bubbly, independent little girl. Rebecca's parents identified the trigger for her difficulties as the birth of a son, Joey, who was described as "outgoing and loving."

A review of family history revealed that Mrs R. grew up as an only child in a house with a lot of screaming and belittling. She called herself a "yeller." She wondered if her daughter's problems came from having always been the center of attention. "Was Rebecca jealous of her brother?" The question was asked in an uncertain manner, as if Mrs R. had difficulty understanding her daughter's feelings. Her general attitude was of disappointment at her daughter's lack of progress. Mrs R. described herself as always having been insecure as a mother and somewhat distant from her children. Rebecca's early development had been reassuring to her. In a similar manner, she now found Joey to be a source of good feelings, while her daughter had let her down. Mrs R. had never enjoyed being at home with the children and had always used full-time caregiving assistance.

Mr R. was antagonistic to treatment. Despite his negativity, however, he was always pleasant with the therapist. What seemed to contribute to his skepticism was an underlying intense emotionality and sensitivity. He was fearful of changing his permissive and somewhat seductive relationship with his daughter. Toward the end of treatment he was able to cooperate with limit-setting established by the mother. Despite the difficulty he had in accepting the need to change, he never actively undermined treatment.

Mr R. described himself as a person who avoided confrontations at all cost. He attributed this characteristic to the fact that he grew up the child of an alcoholic father. He always felt the need to protect his mother from criticism, and he felt similarly protective toward his daughter, whom he perceived as vulnerable. He was fearful of placing demands on her and was cautious because "she might break up." He described his daughter as "spacy." "She blocks things out, shows no real commitment to anything and quits easily." He felt Rebecca was insecure, always searching for attention and love. She seemed to him to have a fear of abandonment: "She doesn't trust us, she has lost her inner security."

In contrast to the mother's uncertainty, Mr R.'s perceptions seemed to be more articulate and empathic. Although inappropriate at times because of his overprotective, intrusive stance, he nonetheless was able to read his daughter's signals of distress. This style of parenting intrigued me, as it reversed the expected pattern of mother–daughter intimacy. I wondered what effect this was having on Rebecca's sense of identity and how this balance of relationships affected oedipal outcome. Did it result in "oedipal victory"? Did it represent a triumph of daughter over mother? Or, alternatively, was her precocious sensuality a defense against yearnings for mother and an underlying feeling of loss? I tended to think the latter dynamics were at work, as Rebecca's sadness became manifest and play themes expressed her sense of loneliness and abandonment. Indeed, her father's role could not compensate for what Rebecca was missing in her relationship with her mother. Mrs R. had already described herself as insecure in her mothering. Was Rebecca somehow trying to compensate for these maternal insecurities at the expense of developing a secure sense of who she was as a separate person?

Parents and Rebecca agreed to a treatment plan of twice-weekly supportive–expressive psychotherapy. Parent counseling sessions were held twice a month. As treatment progressed, the frequency of parent sessions declined to once a month. Treatment for Rebecca extended over a two-year period. Throughout this time the family's treatment alliance with the therapist remained strong.

The Beginning Phase of Treatment

At our first meeting, I encountered a petite, attractive, intense, composed child who sat maturely on the couch and began to enumerate her problems, from time to time receding from direct eye contact and diverting her gaze. She was afraid to go to other people's houses and had big, sad feelings that made her sigh and cry. I noted that Rebecca's parents had not mentioned depression or sadness, only withdrawal and "spaciness." Were both parents out of synch with this aspect of their daughter's subjective experience?

The first phase of treatment consisted almost entirely of non-play activity. Rebecca's capacity to play seemed eclipsed by her assimilation of "grown-up" icons, leaving her no room for self-expression. Our first encounter was telling. Rebecca informed me that she intended to be a writer. There was virtually no delineation of boundary between her expression of purpose and her expectation of achievement. Aspiration and attainment were one. Rebecca asked me for pencil and paper and began to write her "novel." She was literally paralyzed and could not bring pencil to paper productively. After agonizing for over half an hour she produced one dangling phrase, "The little girl…" As Rebecca sat immobile in front of her assigned task, she became frustrated and wondered aloud how she would ever become a writer. My many efforts toward diversion went unheeded; Rebecca was determined not just to write but to become a writer. Her frustration and disappointment became enormous, but she continued to sit diligently in front of the blank paper. Over the course of several sessions I was able to suggest to her that the stories she had inside might emerge more easily if she were able to tell me about her life.

Rebecca spoke of Donna, her teenage baby-sitter, whom she idealized. Donna shared with Rebecca intimacies of her romances and allowed Rebecca to watch sexy movies. Rebecca later confided that she had a fantasy twin named Donna, who was her constant companion. I experienced an almost immediate feeling of being valued as a trusted confidant.

Rebecca spoke openly about her brother Joey, toward whom she had ambivalent feelings. "I cried when mother went to the hospital. He used to be so cute and nice, but not anymore. He's mean and hits me and doesn't share toys with me." This complaint of transformation seemed to echo the parents' description of Rebecca's change from cute baby to problem three-year-old. Rebecca continued, "He hurts me sometimes by saying 'I don't like you.' He just says it to make me feel bad." Her main worry was that when her mother went away, she might not come back, a worry that started when she was six years old. She felt it might never get better.

Rebecca's response to my expression of interest in her was almost immediate. She returned to our next session with several ambivalent impressions of therapy and me. She shared a dream: "I dreamt you were mean and you were going to take me away and steal me." I viewed this dream as the activation of her inner world. She was ready to share this aliveness, though it was confined to states of consciousness where the self was dormant, "asleep" to its everyday experience. She dared to dream I was mean, wanting to take her away and steal her. The dream could be interpreted as a wish that, indeed, I would take her away from her parents and coerce her to be with me. Perhaps more to the point, it was a communication to me about relationship. Rebecca's understanding of relationships was of master/servant enslavement. To be with me would not be her choice; it would be a condition imposed upon her from which there was no escape.

In our meetings I saw Rebecca's frightened side; she would hold on to her coat, for instance. I saw her forceful, coercive side when she pleaded with her mother to stay and then ignored her. She instructed her mother not to yell in the car. She reported that she was not "really" scared at her friend's house. She informed me that her mother said she did not have to come here again and that she would not be returning.

At this point, Rebecca engaged in her first play activity. She drew two pictures, one on the front, the other on the back of the paper. The image on one side was of a woman in slacks; she appeared rigid, defiant, and angry. On the other side was a beautiful, smiling young woman with long hair and flowing dress. Both figures were sparsely depicted, with minimal elaboration. I shared with Rebecca that these pictures were two very different images, the idealized princess of royalty and the frightening, hostile figure (later in therapy to be elaborated as the bad witch).

During this early phase in treatment Rebecca preferred non-play activity. She would engage me in long descriptions of events at school. According to Rebecca, the other kids were "mean" to her. Bobby said her father had died and made her cry. Trisha hit her and lied. When children in class misbehaved, the teacher put their names on the blackboard, causing her great apprehension. Whenever she met new people she worried that they might be "mean." Rebecca used the word "mean" to refer to a broad category of people and experiences she considered unacceptable. These included her brother, some peers, her mother, and at times her therapist. Her father escaped this classification.

Rebecca's sessions revealed additional evidence of her representational world as sharply divided between the "good" and the "bad." One day she told of a bad dream she had had that morning. "I went to the doctor, I was really sick. The doctor was just coming out; I was locked in the hospital. I was crying and screaming for half an hour. There was a fire and I wouldn't let go of the doctor. Then, he let me out of the hospital and I got to go home." Rebecca's fear of the doctor barely concealed a wish that the doctor might keep her with him. It echoed the earlier dream of being "stolen" by me. She was imprisoned, locked in, held against her volition, a relationship based on coercion. She feared the fiery intensity of her feelings. Could these be her "mean" feelings, which the doctor might discover, revealing the ugliness inside her? Clearly, in the dream, Rebecca hoped for a cure and a speedy return to her home. In her therapy, Rebecca was hoping for a rescue from her dilemma of imprisonment. Was the imprisonment imposed upon her by family demands, or was the imprisonment the result of her own rigid and tormenting expectations?

Rebecca was grown-up in her demeanor as she described her problems. She was articulate and offered her own self-prescriptions. For instance, she gave me her remedy for not having bad dreams: "If I can convince myself not to worry, then the bad dream won't come back." Her question to me was "Do grownups ever get sad?" She felt she was bad because she cried and was different from others.

Rebecca wondered if grown-ups were ever sad. In her experience adults had been unable to contain and mirror her feelings of disappointment and sadness. D. W. Winnicott (1963) and others (Beebe & Lachmann 1988; Bion 1962; Emde & Sorce 1983; Stern 1985) have emphasized the importance of parental mirroring of their child's affective states. This attunement enables the child to define himself via the parent's capacity for reverie and introspection. I reflected how deficient Rebecca's upbringing had been in this regard. At first she was overvalued, and then she was devalued with no support for development of her own authentic sense of self-esteem. Perhaps Rebecca's immediate connection to me reflected this lack of authentic relationship to her parents. How would she make use of the therapeutic opportunities now available to her?

DESCRIPTIVE ANALYSIS OF THE PLAY ACTIVITY

In the beginning phase of treatment Rebecca gave only a brief glimpse into her imaginary life. Most of the time in treatment was invested in complaints about school, peers, her parents, her sibling, and the therapist. She could not play; play activity was inhibited by rigid expectations of herself. She longed to be a creative individual but strove to be creative in ways far beyond her chronological abilities. Unrealistic wishes and corresponding fears impeded the flow and spontaneity integral to play activity. In the guise of dreams (non-play), Rebecca allowed herself some self-expression. These dreams condensed the essence of bondage and imprisonment.

In contrast, by using art activity Rebecca was able to give two antagonistic images center stage. She did not perceive them as interacting in any way; they were not in conflict and did not exist as simultaneous images in time. Rather, these two young women existed sequentially, one following the other. Each had its own integrity and its own reality. Each had its separate place in time *(splitting)*. The brief segment of play activity occurred in the macrosphere of the everyday world. It was initiated by Rebecca and inhibited by her through the use of avoidance. Despite the efforts of the therapist to facilitate further unfolding of the play, Rebecca refused to continue to draw and ended the play, seemingly satiated, and went on to non-play (further complaints about the kids at school). The entire play segment took place in the macrosphere.

STRUCTURAL ANALYSIS OF THE PLAY ACTIVITY

Affective Components

During this brief play activity segment, Rebecca's overall hedonic tone was sober. The spectrum of affects expressed was constricted, and the regulation of affective states very rigid. There were no transitions between affective states during this brief segment. The transition into drawing had been spontaneous and abrupt, but there was no accompanying change in affective state. Feelings Rebecca expressed while drawing included aloofness and wariness. There was no evidence of the feelings of fear, worry, or anxiety that were expressed in non-play dialogues and dream states. Rebecca's affective tone was appropriate to the content of the drawing, though as noted it was not expressive. Her feelings for the therapist were generally neutral and at moments somewhat positive. The therapist's attitude towards Rebecca was generally positive.

Cognitive Components

Role representation consisted of dyadic roles (simple collaborative role-play) with the depiction of two characters. The characters were not enlivened with dialogue. Crayons and paper were used in a realistic way and represented realistic objects. There were no transformations of representations (persons or objects) in the play.

Narrative Components

Narrative components were not elaborated in the play activity. No topic or theme of the play activity was explicitly described. The relationship portrayed was only of the self, as the two images were independent of each other. There was an implied relationship involving issues of control (idealized versus demonized), never made explicit. Rebecca was silent for the most part; there was a bare minimum of language used to identify the characters. The therapist used language to describe the drawn images, attempting to ascribe meaning to the play activity.

Developmental Components

The developmental level of the play was somewhat immature because of its constriction. The drawings were of girls; therefore, the gender identity of the play activity was predominantly feminine. Rebecca was initiating play activity on her own, a beginning evidence of practicing efforts towards separation–individuation. For the most part, however, her activity implied yearning for symbiotic merger—between the two girls and with the therapist, who would understand the meaning of her drawings without the need for words to communicate. The social level of Rebecca's play was predominantly solitary (aware), with some cooperation in sharing the drawings with the therapist.

FUNCTIONAL ANALYSIS OF THE PLAY ACTIVITY

In this brief play activity segment, Rebecca demonstrated the *adaptive* use of art materials and minimal *affiliation* with the therapist. Conflict was evident only in the *avoidance* of further elaboration about her work.

Most evident in the drawing were rigid/polarized defenses, including the use of *splitting* (drawing of two women), *idealization* (woman with long hair and flowing dress), and *devaluation* (woman in slacks). There was no evidence of extreme anxiety/isolated play strategies.

Rebecca was consistently aware of her inability to play. She was also painstakingly aware of the first surge toward play activity. Rebecca's finely tuned awareness of her own feeling states and incapacity to perform were prominent markers of her rigidly held emotional state, a state she experienced as precarious and fraught with dangers.

The Middle Phase of Treatment

The middle phase of treatment was marked by a shift in focus within treatment sessions from primarily non-play to primarily play activity. Rebecca used therapy as a safe haven to create a fantasy world inhabited by myriad characters. Within our relationship she seemed to have ended her intense search for a durable, nonretaliating playmate. For me, she had become an active, energized partner in the business of playing. The play took the form of enacting lively interacting roles.

DESCRIPTIVE ANALYSIS OF THE PLAY ACTIVITY

Little Annie, from the comics, was a favored character. She had no friends, only a dog for companionship. She would seek shelter within an orphanage. But even there, refuge was not to be found. Annie might be placed with "mean" foster parents!

At other times, Rebecca would be the mean old witch and command the therapist to have her baby for her, so she could steal it and sell it, as she was too old to have a baby herself. This phenomenon of the witch is a familiar image, representing a cluster of emotional responses (Lane & Chazan 1989). It was recurrent in Rebecca's play. In the world of magic, there are two kinds of witches, good and bad. The good witch has good magic, implicitly knows who we are, and grants us our deepest wishes. The bad witch has bad magic, is childless, and creates terror. Each image is split off from the whole, while its counterpart exists in the unconscious (very much like the two girls drawn by Rebecca in the first phase of treatment).

Rebecca's witch was the hag, an old woman, badly dressed with stringy hair, spindly legs, and a cackling voice. An example of her play follows:

> "Remember your homework? Have sex—have a baby! You have until moonstroke. If you don't do it (approaches me menacingly as if to penetrate me with her knife), I will cut off your head. I have returned with my blade. Have you had a baby? Yes? Then, let me see it. No? Because you didn't have one. I'm sure you'll taste good for dinner. Next time there will be no second chance. Ha—ha! Did you have sex? Good! In nine months you are to have a baby, or else—the blade! I need it for my baby delivering shop. If you don't have it, you will be killed. So, you will work on it, sweetie? I'm too old to have babies. I sell babies. I take them away from people. Since I have helped you and the princess make gold out of straw, you have to give me your firstborn."

This is a phallic old witch, with a long nose, a broomstick between her legs, and a sharp blade. Unable to have children herself, a punishment for her meanness, ugliness, and old age, she is reduced to robbing and stealing. This is the vindictive fantasy of an oedipal little girl, mired in preoedipal conflicts. She cannot forgive her mother for having a baby, and because of her envy and rage she cannot identify with maternal nurturance and life-giving qualities. Doubtless there are also direct transference implications in the depiction of the mean old witch (like the doctor in the dream) who steals children, locks them up, and takes them away from their parents. Wishes and fears are closely intertwined in this characterization.

Absent from this narrative is the fantasized prince who arrives on his white horse just in time to save the damsel in distress. The old woman incorporates menacing phallic features, and a prince is nowhere in sight. He has vanished; just as Rebecca's idealized role dissipated with the birth of Joey, he has been banished, never to return. Sex is degrading, dirty, and demeaning—commanded, but not longed for. And Rebecca magically abandons the beauty of youth, skipping two generations backwards to become the old hag of a witch!

In addition to the bad witch and the beautiful princess, Rebecca introduced many other characters: Dr F., who ran the orphanage, the Queen, the Madam, the Gypsy lady, Cinderella (forced to servitude, who became transformed into the princess by—at last—the arrival of her prince), and Annie (condensing the themes of the "injured" one, the "lost" one, and the "abandoned" one). By playing all of these roles, by reversing play roles, and by playing out intense cannibalistic and aggressive affects, Rebecca began to forge connections between the "split-off" aspects of herself. As she began to heal, object constancy developed. The threat of stealing and being stolen came to an end with the consolidation of superego identifications. A siren would sound, warning that protection was needed. The players reliably heard and responded to its message.

Gone was the haughty demeanor that kept Rebecca aloof from relationship. With the creation of her pantheon of characters, Rebecca developed a more vibrant and spontaneous style of relating. The diversity of characters reflected a growing sense of the varied possibilities for telling a story and having fun. Most important of all, Rebecca clearly perceived herself to be a player, a competent player, capable of creating characters and evolving narratives that had a beginning, a middle, and an end. The activity of play had enabled her to reflect upon and reexperience the misattunements of her early childhood, while continuing the important process of growing.

Rebecca's play activity was rich in its narrative liveliness and diversity, as the above description demonstrates. She spontaneously initiated fantasy play and enjoyed imitating the diverse characters, bringing them vividly to life. Therapist and child jointly facilitated the play, which flowed with no inhibition. There were no disruptions or interruptions in the play. The play activity was usually ended by Rebecca with satiation. The play scenes always took place in the macrosphere.

STRUCTURAL ANALYSIS OF THE PLAY ACTIVITY

Affective Components

Rebecca's feeling state was consistently one of obvious pleasure while playing. Her range of feelings expressed while playing was very wide; these feelings included anger, aggression, anxiety, contempt, curiosity, disgust, envy, worry, and pleasure. Transitions between affective states fluctuated; at times they were smooth, at other times they were abrupt. Overall, Rebecca's emotional regulation was as expected. Her affective tone was usually appropriate to the content of the play. The feelings between therapist and child were mutually very positive.

Cognitive Components

Rebecca represented complex roles in her play, including complex collaborative role-play (three or more interacting parts), directorial play, and narrator play. Representations of people were generally stable. Some transformations occurred voluntarily within a character (for instance, Cinderella). Objects were represented as consistently stable. Play objects were used realistically. The style of representing play objects and people was at times realistic, but usually a mixture of magic and fantasy.

Narrative Components

Rebecca's play contained many topics, including fairy tales, killer, torturer, the Caught One, the One Who Leaves. Themes expressed in the dynamics of the play activity included bodily damage, breaking rules, sexual activities, torture, competition, and servitude. With the arrival of the prince and Daddy Starbucks, the level of relationship within the play narrative became oedipal. Qualities of relationship portrayed within the play narrative ranged from autonomous to malevolent control to destruction by an identifiable agent. Using play activity as a medium of expression had released a Pandora's box of characters and fantasies into Rebecca's play. In place of inhibition there was vivid interaction and portrayal of a wide variety of emotional states, often with an intensity surprising for such a young child.

Rebecca's use of language included verbalization of multiple roles, talking within the metaphor, talking about the meaning of the play, and talking to describe the play. The therapist's use of language included talking within the metaphor and talking about the meaning of the play. Rebecca was using her verbal abilities to complement her fluid, creative, imaginary play.

Developmental Components

Rebecca's play activity was very advanced for her chronological age. There was no predominance in gender identity of the play. Separation–individuation phases represented in the play included elements of practicing (various roles), rapprochement (for example, Annie's threatened return to the orphanage), and constancy (Annie's finding a home). In interactions with the therapist, the social level of the play was reciprocal and cooperative.

FUNCTIONAL ANALYSIS OF THE PLAY ACTIVITY

Rebecca was consistently aware of herself as playing. She exhibited a full range of adaptive coping strategies in the play activity, including *adaptation* (of materials in the play room to her play), *sublimation* (in the stories that clearly expressed her own strivings for acceptance and recognition), *affiliation* (interaction with the therapist), *identification* (with the therapist), and *humor*. Conflicted coping/defensive play strategies were not evident in the play activity. In her fantasy narratives many of the rigid/polarized defenses that had formerly had such a pervasive influence on her life appeared in the guise of play characters. These defensive strategies included *identification with the aggressor, splitting, idealization, projective identification* and *devaluation*.

Projective identification involves more boundary confusion than projection. In projection, an attribute is assigned to another; in projective identification, what is assigned to the other person is an unacceptable, aggressive aspect of the self. Rebecca's characters (Annie, Cinderella, the witch, the doctor, and so on) represented split-off attributes of Rebecca herself. The feared characters (such as the witch) were not only identifications with her parents but also expressions of Rebecca's own unintegrated aggressive impulses. As such these characters were not simply characters; they were aspects of Rebecca that she could recognize and confront in fantasy form. To the extent that creating these characters facilitated Rebecca's personal integration, they were also adaptive and furthered the process of sublimation. In this way, play activity provided a safe haven for exploration and experimentation with feelings and thoughts that otherwise would have remained polarized and rigid. Within the context of play activity, these characters were no longer scary but became fun, intriguing, interesting, and absorbing.

No extreme/isolated anxiety strategies were observed.

The Ending Phase of Treatment
DESCRIPTIVE ANALYSIS OF THE PLAY ACTIVITY

During the ending phase of treatment themes of rejection continued. This time these negative themes emerged in counterpoint to themes of birth. Through her play activity, Rebecca regained her own capacity for creativity and her fantasized capacity for procreation. The oedipal dilemma was resolved by the little girl's relinquishing of her father as romantic consort, her acceptance of the generational divide, her capacity to endure separation and exclusion, and her reunion with her mother. A very vivid play episode depicted Rebecca's resolution of these issues. Following is the description of the play activity as recorded in process notes.

> Rebecca lies on the floor writhing with pain. In the midst of loud screams and grunting noises she gives birth successively to three babies. (How much has Rebecca taken in about sexuality and birth from her teenage caregiver? Has she ever seen pictures or a film of birthing?) The first is black and is given up for adoption. The second is kept for only a few days. The third baby she cuddles and sings to with great warmth, even though she has green eyes. Birth and acceptance of this third baby seem to signify self-acceptance, as well as identification with the nurturing maternal role.

The resolution of Rebecca's narcissistic dilemma was seen in her entrance into latency with a renewed sense of happiness and industry. She became an active entrepreneur. She produced bracelets and lanyards, began a business selling chocolates, eagerly anticipated and enjoyed playdates, and invested effort in schoolwork. As these other interests emerged, our lively play characters receded from view. Once again, our time together was spent primarily in non-play, conversation about her daily activities and events occurring within the family and in school.

The ending of treatment occurred gradually over a period of three months. As the frequency of sessions diminished, I found myself reflecting upon the powerful effects of play activity on development, as if the capacity to play, "playfulness," can become synonymous with the capacity for humanness and relationship.

The analysis of the play activity in the ending phase of treatment focuses upon the play segments depicting the birth of Rebecca's three fantasy babies. She played out these ideas in fantasy, using imitation of the birth process, jazz singing, and art activity (drawing the babies). The play was initiated spontaneously by Rebecca, who also gave suggestions to the therapist as to how to play her role. Play activity was facilitated by both therapist and child; there was no evidence of inhibition. Play activity was ended by Rebecca when she was satiated. There were no disruptions or interruptions of the play activity. All of the play was enacted in the macrosphere.

STRUCTURAL ANALYSIS OF THE PLAY ACTIVITY

Affective Components

During the play activity Rebecca's overall feeling was of obvious pleasure; her spectrum of affects was very wide. Affects expressed in the play included aggression, anger, anxiety, contempt, curiosity, disgust, envy, worry, elation, and pleasure. Transition between feeling states was usually smooth, with some abruptness due to dramatic effects. Rebecca's regulation and modulation of feelings were somewhat flexible, and the feelings expressed in the play were appropriate to the content of the play. Rebecca and her therapist became bonded through the play and shared very warm and affectionate feelings.

Cognitive Components

Rebecca's play was intricate and emotional. She used several interacting characters in her play (complex collaborative role-play), and she directed the play. Persons represented remained stable; neither persons nor objects underwent transformation. Play objects were used realistically for the most part, but occasionally Rebecca would substitute a different object to represent something else. This capacity for symbolization enlarged the domain of the play activity. Both persons and objects in the play had elements of fantasy and reality.

Narrative Components

In Rebecca's play, birth occurred in the presence of a doctor and a jazz singer. She set the scene in a fantasy setting that had the atmosphere of a fairy tale. The play was about birth and the process of giving birth, caregiving, rejection, and separation. Relationships between characters in the story were depicted as both autonomous (adults) and dependent (infants). Rebecca was very verbal in the play. She communicated using sounds (during the birth) and language to verbalize several roles, to talk within the metaphor of the play, and to describe the play. The therapist used language to speak within the metaphor of the play and to talk about the meaning of the play.

Developmental Components

The developmental level of the play was very advanced for Rebecca's chronological age. The play was predominantly feminine, based around issues of giving birth. The adult characters in the story had all achieved the level of constancy. Interaction with the therapist (social level of the play) was reciprocal and cooperative.

FUNCTIONAL ANALYSIS OF THE PLAY ACTIVITY

Adaptive strategies used in the play activity included *adaptation, problem-solving, sublimation, affiliation, identification*, and *humor*. Some evidence of conflict was observed in the use of *repression* to ward off fears of giving birth; also, sexual feelings were *projected* onto the character of the jazz singer, and nurturance onto the character of the doctor.

Rigid/polarized defenses observed were minimal; *identification with the aggressor* was used in the rejection of two of the babies. There was no use of extreme anxiety/isolated defense strategies in the play activity.

Rebecca was consistently aware that she was playing and joyful in her new assertive capacity.

Rebecca's CPTI Profiles Over Treatment

Segmentation revealed sharp differences among the three phases of Rebecca's treatment. At the point of entry into treatment, Rebecca engaged primarily in non-play activity, talking with the therapist about her difficulties. During the beginning phase there was only one occurrence of play activity; it was brief, yet expressive of Rebecca's underlying relationship issues. Play activity was inhibited because of unrealistic demands on herself for performance. The middle phase of treatment was dramatically different.

Rebecca's activity was predominantly play activity. As her trust in the therapeutic relationship deepened, she was able to express herself through the
voices of various characters in dramatic play. The ending phase of treatment
returned to a predominance of non-play and art projects. Rebecca became
industrious, gregarious, and fun-loving. The play activity segment
analyzed dealt with birth and rejection, major themes in her search for
identity. By the conclusion of treatment, coping strategies were predominantly adaptive. The shift in strategies from rigid/polarized to characteristically adaptive is seen in Figure 4.1.

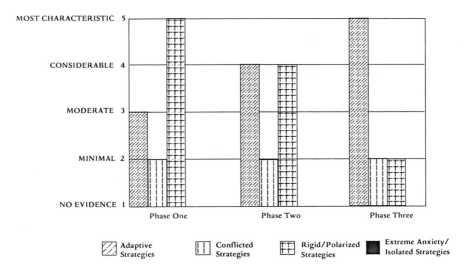

Figure 4.1 Rebecca's Coping–Defensive Strategies in the Course of Treatment

For Rebecca "the play was the thing." Most issues were worked out in the
play activity itself, not in direct interaction with the therapist. The play
contained the sensitive feelings, allowing them to emerge without the
threat of retaliation. Within the play activities polarities were integrated.
Rebecca came to therapy predominantly introverted. Her rigid overcontrol
and fear of her feelings held a submerged, vital emotional life disguised as
aloofness. She left therapy a freer, more confident and playful person.

   The story of Rebecca illustrates how early injury within the parent–
child dyad prevents healthy differentiation and integration. Rebecca's difficulties were rooted in failures of parental attunement, mirroring, and con-

tainment. In addition, Rebecca was at risk because of her extreme constitutional sensitivity to the reactions of others. Her sensitivity was not balanced by sufficient affect regulation and modulation. Rather, her sensitivities left her emotionally labile and vulnerable. Because of her intense, unmodulated feelings, she resorted to the use of maladaptive defenses, including splitting, avoidance, and projective identification. These maladaptive defenses led to estrangement and loneliness, the very feelings she feared. Aggression aroused by maladaptive interaction with others was taken by Rebecca as anger against herself, and she became sad.

Rebecca's perception of herself as unworthy of love, as a slave to superior beings (or the reverse, entitled to limitless love and admiration, empowered over others), was portrayed through play activity. These images had been shared by parents and child on an unconscious level. Avoidance of authentic interaction between parents and child maintained the salience of these fantasized relationships, images that became enshrined in Rebecca's subjective world as immutable realities.

In Rebecca's play activity, themes of revenge and birth captured the options of life and death. Living would mean to be less than perfect; dying would be an embodiment of rigid parental expectations. In this sense, Rebecca's initial encapsulation in narcissism was submission to her own and her parents' harsh edict that she did not have a right to a full life. Instead, she led an idealized existence, enslaved to false values and self-absorption. As she confronted latency, these narcissistic defenses crumbled, giving full expression to Rebecca's inner despair. With this encounter with disillusionment, therapeutic engagement became a possibility and cleared the impasse to developmental progress.

Clinical Case: Anna and Her Therapeutic Baby

In contrast to Rebecca's state of inhibition, the second clinical case to be described illustrates how a low tolerance for frustration and poor control of impulses can result in a reduced capacity for adaptability in play activity. Although some of the major defenses Anna used in play activity—rigid/polarized strategies—were similar in form to those used by Rebecca, her capacity to cope and her ability to form relationships with others were, at time of referral, markedly deficient.

Anna, the younger of two siblings living in an intact urban middle-class family, was six years old at the time of referral for treatment. She experienced extreme negativism and fears, uncontrolled outbursts of aggression, and interpersonal difficulties with family and peers. Anna met all six summary criteria for the diagnosis of borderline child (Vela, Gottlieb, and Gottlieb 1983).

Review of family relationships revealed an unsettled environment, partially in response to Anna and her difficulties, partially reflecting marital disharmonies, and partially reflecting external extended-family and financial pressures. Anna's developmental history revealed that although a second child had been planned for "sometime in the future," her conception was unanticipated and occurred at a time when Mrs A. felt overwhelmed by the demands of mothering. Pregnancy and labor were normal. Anna was breast-fed for four months. Sometime during the first year, she began to reject her mother, turning her head away from an offered kiss or embrace. Motor and language milestones were within normal limits. Toilet training was spontaneous at about two years. Beginning at age three, Anna attended a two-day nursery program, then at age four proceeded to a five-day program. Separation problems did not appear until later in kindergarten and began insidiously as dawdling when getting ready for school. By first grade, departure from home was a source of ongoing stress and hostility between mother and child.

The Beginning Phase of Treatment

Although Anna welcomed her therapy hours, she was slow to engage in play activity. She noted the toys and talked about them positively; she also noted that the therapist had a dog, and she associated to other dogs she had known. She preferred the non-play of conversation; talking seemed safe and a way to maintain control. Following this brief honeymoon period of cooperation, Anna became increasingly attacking and oppositional. Direct physical attacks alternated with wild mean looks and periods of puppet play depicting sadistic patterns between a king and a queen. This was an intense period of confusion, with marked ambivalence toward me, as Anna tried to fend me off by perceiving me as frightening.

In one session, we worked with watercolors. There was good control, with only a bit of spilling. Anna painted a hill with a circle on top, then covered the painting with water, making the picture fade away. On another sheet she muddled the colors together. I interpreted these colors as her confused feelings, the reason she was coming to therapy. Each time she made a mess of the colors in the box, she would ask my assistance to tidy them up.

Anna: Where does the yellow go?

(I link the colors with feelings and suggest that when we work together feelings become clearer and less confused. Anna asks for a larger piece of paper and then tears it up with a malicious smile. I ask her if she can use the parts. She checks her watch and comments that mine is fast by three minutes. I agree to follow hers)

Anna: The parts are too small. *(Starts tearing smaller and smaller pieces. In a baby voice)* Too small…too small.

Therapist: A little baby sometimes feels the world is a confusing place—everything seems to run together. It's good to have a place to bring those baby feelings.

(Anna, with a twinkle in her eye, goes to the blackboard and asks my assistance in spelling the word "humorous." She proceeds to write the word humorous over and over again on the blackboard. She adds my name and writes, "Saralea is humorous.")

Therapist: Yes, I am pretty funny, but maybe even a bit scary, too.

(Anna draws my face very clearly, then erases the features and makes them jagged with lightning flashes)

Therapist: Sometimes I am humorous and it feels comfortable with me; sometimes I am humorous and I have a lightning face. It can be very confusing here.

During the next session, smiling maliciously Anna threw a ball directly at me. I said this hurt me and directed her to a doll instead. She immediately accepted the surrogate object and created a game of throwing balls at the doll and keeping score.

Therapist:	The doll does not have its own feelings, or otherwise it would be hurt.
Anna:	The doll is humorous. It likes getting hurt.
Therapist:	No one likes getting hurt; that's why we have toys to play with.
Anna:	*(Examines anus of doll and pulls its legs apart)* The vagina would be here. This kind of doll takes water from a bottle. The water comes out the back, but the bottle is lost. We could put the water in its mouth.

As this session ended, I noted some anxious clinging to me at separation.

At a session the following week, at my suggestion we began with messy pasting play. Anna used up a small bottle of glue pasting tissues into a large wad.

Therapist:	It's fun to bring all of your messy feelings into therapy. Somehow they are all holding together, but we have run out of supplies.

(Anna begins kicking therapist. Therapist directs Anna to doll. Anna throws down the doll and stands on top of it)

Therapist:	Do you think she likes being thrown down and getting hurt?

(Anna writes on sheet of paper: "You are humorous.")

Therapist:	That means you think I like getting hurt. No one likes getting hurt. These feelings come on so suddenly. At first you enjoy messy feelings, and then they become frightening—suddenly you felt attacked.
Anna:	*(Begins a game of catch with the doll)* Who is that? Really me?
Therapist:	Who is that? Really Anna?
Anna:	*(Hits the baby doll on the head four times, counting)* One. Two. Three. Four.

Therapist: Big girl Anna and baby Anna. When big girl Anna hits baby Anna, does big girl Anna hurt baby Anna? It seems like big girl Anna is confused. She thinks that if her baby is hit, she will feel better. I think it hurts. Did anyone ever hit you this way?

(Anna shakes her head. She takes a large sheet of paper and draws a whole figure—a snowman)

The doll (baby Anna) became a prominent attachment figure for Anna. One day she came in very upset. A statue she saw on the way to my office had been covered with paint on mischief night. She began to paint and painted off the paper, seemingly unaware of the mess. She responded to limit-setting by attacking me. I explained mischief night to Anna, who claimed that if children attacked her car, she would throw apples out the window. She then returned to the play activity, repeatedly letting the baby Anna fall. Anna painted bruises on the doll.

Therapist: Poor doll. She keeps falling down and getting hurt. Poor doll, you are pushing her down. She doesn't like it. It hurts. This is a very, very precious baby. She is humorous. She has a high spirit and many, many needs. She needs a lot of care. Maybe she would rather get a hug than a hit. Maybe the baby is getting hit because she can't get a hug. A humorous baby is one you can hug.

(Anna gradually stops throwing the baby doll and, making eye contact with me, she holds baby Anna close. Then Anna feeds baby Anna until she has had enough)

DESCRIPTIVE ANALYSIS OF THE PLAY ACTIVITY

Although Anna was cautious about beginning play activity, she did engage in the categories of art activity, game play, and fantasy play. Her play activity was subject to disruption as aggressive impulses broke through. In those moments, the play activity was marginal and occasionally crossed the boundary to become non-play. Play activity was usually initiated by the therapist; it was facilitated by both Anna and therapist. Anna inhibited the play by refusing to play. Play activity was ended by Anna at times with satiation, at times with disruption, and at times by transition to non-play activity; the therapist ended the play at times with limit-setting. The sphere of the play was completely within the macrosphere.

STRUCTURAL ANALYSIS OF THE PLAY ACTIVITY

Affective Components

Anna's feelings fluctuated over a wide range between pleasurable interest and overt distress. Her regulation and modulation (control) of her feelings was usually somewhat rigid, with transitions between affective states usually abrupt (like lightning). Feelings expressed by Anna in her play included aggression, anger, curiosity, fear, pleasure, anxiety, and wariness. At most times her feelings expressed were appropriate for the content played; exceptions were due to outbursts of aggression and maliciousness. Anna was never neutral in her attitude toward the therapist; her feelings toward her varied from very positive to very negative. Anna's therapist was somewhat positive in relating to her.

Cognitive Components

Anna's role-play was on the level of dyadic representation (simple collaborative play); Anna used the doll as a partner and also engaged puppets in dyadic interaction. Representations of people were usually stable, but these representations were also subject to voluntary transformations (the intense ambivalence of "humorous"). Representations of objects appeared to be generally stable. Upon close scrutiny, however, in her initial use of watercolors Anna seemed to be expressing aspects of the experience of involuntary transformation with fluid representation. Similarly, her concern with the statues being painted (non-play dialogue) was with the issue of involuntary transformation and fluid representation. This tendency to perceive objects as marginally transforming communicates the subtle, intense edge to Anna's states of anxiety. Despite these anxieties, play objects were generally used realistically. People were represented at times realistically, at times with fantasy attributes; representation of objects was generally realistic.

Narrative Components

The topic of Anna's play was fighting; themes expressed in the play included bodily damage, caregiving, messing, and hurting. Within the narrative the level of relationships depicted was dyadic, representing interpersonal events between two parties. The character of relationships portrayed vacillated between dependency, malevolent control, and destruction by an identifiable object. Language used by Anna in the play included verbalization of a single role, talking within the metaphor, and talking describing the play. Language used by the therapist in the play included talking within the metaphor, talking about the meaning of the play, and talking describing the play.

Developmental Components

Anna's play activity was somewhat immature because of impulses breaking through the organization of her play. The play activity reflected no predominance of gender role. Very early issues of separation–individuation were observed, including differentiation (funny/scary; confusion of colors) and practicing (trying out the expression of her feelings within a new relationship). In interaction with her therapist Anna at times played alone, aware of her therapist's presence; at other moments she would engage in reciprocal interaction. Even during intense moments of aggressive outbursts there was give and take in communication between therapist and child. Anna was attuned to the clarifications of the therapist, if not always able to modulate her response.

FUNCTIONAL ANALYSIS OF THE PLAY ACTIVITY

In this initial phase of treatment Anna was only minimally aware of herself as playing. The boundary between playing and acting out of impulses was unclear. Because of this confusion, play activity could not be experienced as secure. Anna's ambivalence toward the therapist was expressed in repeated testing of the limits of the play. Clarifications by the therapist seemed to ameliorate this confused state, which could become overwhelming for Anna.

Adaptive strategies in the play included the beginning use of *affiliation* (with the therapist) and *identification* (with the therapist). Conflicted strategies were not observed in the play. The predominant strategies observed were rigid/polarized defensive strategies. These defensive strategies included *splitting* (therapist's face as humorous, then frightening), *projective identification* (the doll likes getting hurt), *identification with the aggressor* (hitting and kicking doll), and *omnipotent control* (wanting to set her own limits). Extreme anxiety/isolated play strategies were minimally observed as *dedifferentiation* and *dispersal* in her messing and scattering of play materials.

The Middle Phase of Treatment

During this phase of treatment the first sustained play activity appeared that was not interrupted by bursts of aggression.

Upon entering the room, Anna chooses to play with small dinosaur figures. The meat-eaters fight each other to "dead" the bird who teases "Come and get me." The plant-eaters take over the world, thanks to the bird. The meat-eaters eat each other up and become extinct. "They are not only dead, they are all gone forever." The dinosaurs are bigger and stronger, but the baby bird can make them chase him and get a lot of attention by teasing and being bad. The bad little bird wants the dinosaurs to chase him. Anna plays at being the bird, jumping up and down on the couch. She lays eggs.

Anna finds a new hiding place under my desk, where she keeps her secrets. She plays she is a jellyfish that stings and hurts while hiding in the ocean. Then she becomes an octopus that continues to eat even after it is dead.

At the next session, from her hiding place Anna told a story about a desert dog who lived in a tent left by explorers. They didn't know they had left her, since she was so very, very tiny—a baby. "I don't want to talk about it." Anna made a drawing. She crossed out the dog and put in eggs instead. The drawing she didn't like she gave to me (but didn't tear up); the drawing she did like she gave to her mother.

In play Anna increasingly became the nurturing one, welcoming me to a tea party and feeding her babies. She began to seek out her mother for security whenever she encountered threatening feelings. Mother's presence was becoming a source of reassurance. New additions to play activities were gymnastics and jump rope skills. Anna practiced these activities and enjoyed performing for me, and I felt entertained.

Several weeks passed, and Anna began a new play activity, this time with a baby doll with hair whom she named David.

Anna:	We'll cut his hair and make him a penis. *(She cuts the penis off and he cries. She pastes it on again)*
Anna:	*(Speaking for David)* I feel weird. I don't have a penis, and I don't have a vagina. I don't know what I am.
Anna:	Be still or I'll cut off your arm. *(To me)* Tell him I'm not serious. My Dad told me when I was very, very little he cut my hair like this. He saved it, but I never saw it.

(We collect the doll's hair and put it in an envelope)

Anna:	*(Turns to the Anna doll)* She hurt the doll. I don't know if it' is a boy or a girl.
Therapist:	This doll hurt itself because it felt different. Its scars are better now.

(Anna looks at the sores she had inflicted on the doll's eyes and decides they are better, too. She says "it" (David) is a boy and hurt his head so he was bleeding; she also draws on new bruises)

At the next session Anna went immediately to the Anna doll and decided it was a girl. She drew a vagina on it, with a clitoris and a place to pee.

Therapist:	Some kids think that if they do not have a penis something is wrong—it fell off, or got lost.
Anna:	It didn't. She's a girl and has a vagina. She knows she doesn't have a penis.

(Anna continues putting sores on the doll because she is "bad." She gives the doll a red rear end and puts multiple hurts on her stomach)

Therapist:	Some kids feel so bad they do not have a penis, they feel they have to hurt themselves; they are so different.
Anna:	Let's clean her up. *(She makes a diaper for baby Anna)*
Therapist:	How did she get hurt?

Anna: Her parents got shot. She jumped off the Empire State Building. She couldn't find her mommy and daddy. They went to the Museum of Natural History and are with the dinosaurs.

Therapist: How terrible it is when parents argue—you feel like they cannot take care of themselves, like something terrible might happen. Anna might lose them and worry it was her fault.

(Anna takes the doll and immerses her totally in water. Then she cleans baby Anna completely and pronounces that she "came out like new." Anna wants her mother to see)

Two weeks later it was Mother's Day. Anna drew a face, my face as she first saw me. Then, she drew a succession of three faces: a composite face of myself and her mother, a frenzied face, and a clown's face. She was intent on showing me the changes in her mother's face and how she was different from me. She was particularly concerned with the mouth and used a mirror to search for her own uvula. We talked about changes that occur from day to day and about differences between people, such as eye color. Anna drew a picture of a "precious little girl." She continued to hide in her tiny space and asked not to be laughed at because she wished to be so small.

Anna: This little girl walks and talks at one second old.

Anna acknowledged that this is unreal. She remembered that when she was little she slept in her parents' room and ate potatoes and applesauce and from her mommy's breast.

Therapist: How did your brother feel about that?

Anna: He did not see me. I was in the crib in mommy's room.

On the blackboard Anna wrote the words, "*I am.*" This was the first session to end with no manifest separation anxiety.

DESCRIPTIVE ANALYSIS OF THE PLAY ACTIVITY

Anna used various categories of play activity, including traumatic play, fantasy play, exploration, and art activity. Anna was the primary initiator of play activity, feeling more comfortable in the play room. Both Anna and the therapist facilitated the play; the play was not inhibited. Play activity was ended primarily by Anna with satiation. Play activity occurred in all three spheres of play—minimally in the autosphere (examining her uvula), moderately in the microsphere (miniature dinosaurs), and predominantly in the macrosphere (dolls, art activity).

STRUCTURAL ANALYSIS OF THE PLAY ACTIVITY

Affective Components

Overall, Anna demonstrated pleasurable interest in the play activity, with some sober moments associated with the cutting of the doll's hair. She expressed a wide spectrum of feelings, including aggression, anger, anxiety, curiosity, envy, fear, and pleasure. Transitions between affective states fluctuated, at times smooth but at other times abrupt. Regulation of feelings was midway between rigid and flexible. Anna's affective expression was usually appropriate to the content of the play. The affective tone between therapist and child was somewhat positive, still tinged with ambivalence.

Cognitive Components

Anna engaged in complex role-play (representing three or more roles). She also engaged in narrator play, where she commented on play events. Despite initial confusion regarding the gender identity of the dolls, stability of representation of both objects and persons was generally maintained, with no transformations.

Although Anna played at taking multiple roles, none of these roles transformed; rather one creature (or person) was substituted for another. An exception occurred in the drawings of faces. Although not explicit, it seemed that Anna was depicting not only the differences between the split images (my and her mother's faces), but also how they underwent transformation to become a frenzied face and then a clown face. These faces did not seem to be separate perceptions. The first image (therapist/mother) was a confabulation; the next two images seemed to some degree to be overlapping and continuous. To the extent that these representations were spontaneous, they were fluid and not entirely voluntary.

Anna's use of play objects was consistently realistic. Her style of representation of objects and persons combined elements of reality and fantasy.

Narrative Components

Fighting (a response to confusion) and the search for identity were the main topics of Anna's play. Themes of the play included bodily damage, bodily function, caregiving, feeding, resurrection, and rebirth. The play contained episodes for two (dyadic) and three (triadic) players. A variety of relationships was portrayed within the narrative, embodying the characteristics of dependence, malevolent control, and destruction by an identifiable agent. There was considerable use of language during the play activity. Anna verbalized multiple roles, talked within the metaphor, described the play, talked about something other than the play, and elucidated its meaning (for example, gender identity of the doll). The therapist used language to talk within the metaphor, describe the play and the meaning of the play, and talk about something other than the play.

Developmental Components

Because of the confusion reflected in Anna's thought processes, the developmental level of her play activity was somewhat immature in organization. Caregiving activities in the play were predominantly feminine; otherwise the play demonstrated no gender dominance. Differentiation and practicing were observed as Anna continued to explore and identify differences (for example, between alive and dead, between devouring and nurturing) and practice her new understandings gained through playing. The social level of the play was reciprocal interaction between Anna and her therapist.

FUNCTIONAL ANALYSIS OF THE PLAY ACTIVITY

During this intermediate phase in treatment there was considerable evidence of Anna's growing awareness of her role as a player. This awareness paralleled Anna's increased sense of her own identity and diminished state of confusion. A strong pull toward relationship with the therapist modified her need to nullify and divorce play activity from meaning. As Anna communicated clearly to the therapist that "you can accept my precious little girl self," she instructed the therapist not to laugh at her wishes, as she knew they were unreal. The strength of the therapeutic bond (reflected in Anna's instructions to the "therapist who listens") seemed to alleviate her previous alienation from strong wishes to be loved as little and dependent.

Adaptive strategies were frequently observed in the play activity. These adaptive play strategies included *affiliation* (with the therapist), *identification* (for example, with the doll's missing parts), emergence of authentic (non-anxiety-based) *humor*. *Projection* and *regression* (conflicted strategies) were major resources for feelings and themes expressed in the play activity.

Rigid/polarized play strategies were still dominant in the play activity. These strategies included *splitting* (meat- from plant-eaters), *projective identification* (explorers leave baby dog, unknowingly), and *identification with the aggressor* (cutting the doll's hair; play at being the "bad" dog). The tendency towards fluidity and multiple percepts described in the discussion of cognitive components suggests an early modification of these embedded rigid strategies. Also to be noted is the absence of disruptions due to loss of impulse control. No extreme anxiety/isolated strategies were observed in the play activity.

The Ending Phase of Treatment

DESCRIPTIVE ANALYSIS OF THE PLAY ACTIVITY

Toward the end of the second year of treatment, Anna visited a medieval museum where she viewed the tapestries of the unicorn. Their portrayal of blood and battle terrified her. In therapy, inspired by the tapestry and its depiction of birds, she created a fantasy world of birds, an activity that was sustained over a three-month period. Each bird was made of a different metal (as were the church treasures in the museum), forming a hierarchy of preciousness. Subsequently, this hierarchy was further refined with a lineage of different-colored birds, each with its distinctive characteristics. In this fantasy world there were also a pair of turtles, a snake, and a vulture. The gold jay would nest and have babies (there were blue jays and cardinals outside my office window). Within this play activity Anna was able to begin to talk about relationships at home, sibling rivalry, and her brother's wish that she were dead.

The death of Anna's pet bird, Bluebird, became an important focus for family interaction. Anna wanted to hold and caress the dead animal. Her father was frightened by these feelings and called me for suggestions and reassurance. A funeral was held, and Anna was permitted to grieve. In therapy she was able to talk about the episode and share her sadness with me. Her fantasy was of rebirth, like a jack-in-the-box. She was angry at Bluebird for leaving. She took out a doll and began caring for it.

Anna: When I grow up I will be a big girl, and then a teenager, then a woman, then a mother; I will need a grandmother and grandmother will need a great-grandmother. Do I have a great-grandmother?

We talked about her awareness of death. Anna talked to me more about Bluebird, saying "I feel completely good about her." It was a moving experience for her parents as well, who took pride in their management of the loss.

Concerns about ending were first expressed at the time of the death of Bluebird. Anna became aware that there might be a time when she would no longer need to come to treatment. Coincidental with these concerns were some definite signs of progress, both within her inner world and with those in the world around her. Anna's fantasies became less tyrannical and punitive. Her characters became playful, and events that had seemed scary now at times could be perceived as amusing. Anna was no longer a passive agent in her play; she willfully imposed outcomes and suggested alternative versions of scripts.

Anna became very involved with the widely publicized case of Baby Fae, an infant who was given an artificial heart. In the therapy room, Baby Susan was born. She suffered from a congenital defect of a split heart that needed to be healed. Baby Susan survived, even in the face of the death of Baby Fae, and was nurtured well by parents and doctors. Within the transference, sadistic projections decreased and there was increased pleasure in being together. Particularly significant was Anna's new-found ability to make reparation: "*I want to apologize. Sometimes when I get angry, that's how I act.*"

These forward steps alternated with regressive periods, recalling the earlier days of treatment. Outbursts of aggression, extreme fearfulness, and physical attacks would indicate the resurgence of old issues. I told Anna that when these frightening concerns came back, I noticed she could now almost take care of them on her own. I reassured her that we would work together on them as long as necessary. Anna created two new games reflecting her understanding of the treatment process. One was called "Looking Forward and Looking Backward"; the other involved discovering the end and beginning of a maze. These games were played spontaneously at different times during the ending phase of treatment, and we were both actively involved in the play.

A new bird to replace the lost bird brought a resurgence of concerns regarding separation. Anna talked about the loss of her old bird, who had eggs; the new one was a male. Anna would sit in my rocking chair with baby Anna alongside her and ask if she could always visit me and if I would visit her. We talked about her wish to be my baby and always be with me. With increased acceptance of the limits of the treatment relationship, our bond strengthened. Anna talked about metamorphosis (a big word!); she defined it as *something transformed that undergoes change like a butterfly or a frog.* The room was her cocoon, and I reflected how comfortable she seemed to feel now in the cocoon while undergoing change. Anna welcomed the new school year, and in early fall we began a gradual disengagement from treatment, with allowance for follow-up sessions as requested.

Anna's play activity included imitation, fantasy, and art activity. Play activity was initiated by Anna and facilitated by both Anna and the therapist. There was no evidence of inhibition of the play activity. Anna usually ended the play activity with satiation; alternatively, she moved on to non-play without satiation (conversations). Although outbursts did occur during the session, they were usually not disruptive to the play activity and occurred as separate non-play segments. The balance of sessions was almost equally divided between play and non-play (mostly talking about everyday events).

Anna's play included a microsphere (a tiny world of birds) of her own creation. Like day residue in a dream, this imaginary world that she constructed had its antecedents in viewing a real work of art. Of note was the transformation of this scary battling world into a pleasurable, ordered, playful sphere of interaction. Considerable play occurred in the macrosphere, the everyday realm, as well. No play occurred in the autosphere (play on the body).

STRUCTURAL ANALYSIS OF THE PLAY ACTIVITY

Affective Components

Anna's overall hedonic tone was predominantly obvious pleasure. The range of feelings expressed was wide, including anxiety, curiosity, fear, sadness, worry, and pleasure. Regulation of affects was somewhat flexible, with transitions between feeling states generally smooth. Anna's affective tone was usually appropriate to the play content. Affective tone expressed between the play participants (therapist and Anna) was very positive.

Cognitive Components

Anna's use of role representations was complex and included narrator play. Roles represented showed various forms of stability. Most representations were stable with no transformations (particularly inanimate objects). Toward the end of treatment, however, there were remarkable instances of voluntary transformations (of persons and animals) to stable representations. In a parallel development, change as part of living and growing could be perceived as nonthreatening progress. These transitions were no longer traumatic, as they were referenced to stable ongoing relationships. In her play Anna used objects realistically. Representations of people and objects were both fantastic and realistic.

Narrative Components

The narrative of Anna's play activity was diverse and rich in variety of characters and events. Battles (fighting), fables, treasures, and doctors were all topics for her play. Themes of Anna's play activity included birth, bodily damage, caregiving, death, illness, metamorphosis, separation, and reparation. Relationships portrayed within the play involved oedipal (familial) dynamics (it was noteworthy that intergenerational references were to a maternal lineage). The characteristics of relationships depicted in the play narrative included autonomy, dependence, and destruction by an identifiable agent. Anna used words to express multiple roles and to speak within the metaphor of the play. In addition she used language to describe the play, to talk about things other than the play, and to convey the meaning of the play. The therapist used language to speak within the metaphor of the play and to converse about the meaning of the play.

Developmental Components

Anna's play was developmentally advanced in its use of extensive metaphor and elaboration of play concepts; there was no predominance in the gender identity of the play. Rapprochement conflicts and constant relationships (separation–individuation) were depicted in Anna's play. Interactions between therapist and Anna (social level) were both reciprocal and cooperative.

FUNCTIONAL ANALYSIS OF THE PLAY ACTIVITY

Anna was consistently aware that she was playing. This observation is consistent with her pleasure in the elaboration of extensive and continuous play narratives (extending over several sessions) and the achievement of individuation (separation–individuation) in play. Adaptive play strategies included *adaptation* (of play materials, regulation of affective states in interaction), *anticipation* (of the ending of the play), *sublimation* (of emotional needs), *affiliation* (with therapist, among characters in the play), *identification* (with the therapist), and authentic (non-anxious) *humor*. Conflicted strategies observed in Anna's play activity included *intellectualization* (her museum interests) and *regression* to infantile neediness.

Rigid/polarized play strategies were not observed within the play activity. During aggressive outbursts in non-play segments when she was interacting with the therapist, there was evidence of continued identification with the aggressor and loss of impulse control. These problematic behaviors reemerged as the ending of treatment became more and more of a reality, as if to test the robustness of therapeutic progress. Within segments of play activity, however, the focus was almost exclusively upon reparation, healing, and metamorphosis to a more mature, integrated state of emotional health. No extreme anxiety/isolated defense strategies were observed within the play activity.

Anna's CPTI Profiles Over Treatment

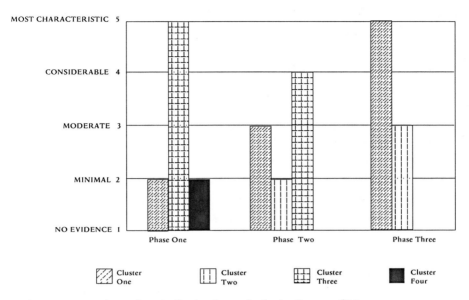

Figure 4.2 Anna's Coping–Defensive Strategies in the Course of Treatment

A global assessment of segmentation over the three phases of treatment (done from process notes; timed intervals were not available) revealed early disruption of play activity due to the eruption of aggressive impulses. Midway in treatment, boundaries within the play session became secure, and play activity flourished. In the ending phase of treatment, the elaboration of play activity and the use of metaphor embellished the play in new ways. Play activity shared a focus with non-play. During periods of non-play, occasional disruptive behaviors reappeared.

The shift in coping/defensive strategies over the course of Anna's treatment is shown in Figure 4.2. The beginning phase profile of coping/defensive strategies in her play activity revealed a predominance of rigid/polarized defenses, with minimal evidence of adaptation and extreme anxiety/isolated strategies. As Anna became more secure within the therapeutic setting and her play activity became more organized, there was a definite diminution in rigid/polarized defenses, with a parallel increase in adaptation and strategies dealing with conflict. By the end of treatment, play activity had advanced significantly, becoming a major secure route for Anna's self-exploration. Rigid/polarized strategies were no longer evident; play strategies observed either were adaptive or conveyed conflictual themes involving regression and intellectualization.

Structural analysis of Anna's play activity clarifies the process by which therapeutic progress was achieved. Progress in treatment was reflected in Anna's greater affective regulation and modulation, cognitive reorganization, and clarification of role representations, as well as demarcation of boundaries between fantasy and reality. The dynamics of play themes became complex, with myriad characters metaphorically resolving overwhelming, terrifying play themes. As Anna's play advanced developmentally, she was able to achieve a cooperative relationship within the transference, as well as within the metaphor of play. These are the gains that account for the significant shifts that occurred in coping–defensive play strategies.

Both Anna's and Rebecca's cases demonstrate the function of play activity as an essential sphere of child development. In the beginning of treatment, inhibition obliterated Rebecca's freedom of exploration of herself and the world around her. In Anna's case, confusion overwhelmed her, resulting in an obliteration of boundaries that kept impulses and wishes apart from thought and action. In order for these traumatic feelings to be modified, they needed to be reenacted in treatment, either directly in the transference relationship or indirectly in play and fantasy.

Interestingly, both Rebecca and Anna used the birth of a child as a central vehicle for their own emotional rebirth. The common use of this metaphor suggests the centrality of gender as an early organizer of the little girl's subjective experience. Gradually, as both children were able to use play as an arena of safety, they were able to gain entrance to a creative representational mode of self-expression. Therapist and child were then able to use language to facilitate the growth of mutual understandings, enabling symbolic process to emerge in the linking of words with feelings.

CHAPTER 5

The Extremely Anxious/ Isolated Player

The extremely anxious/isolated child plays in a manner that is personal and often idiosyncratic. The degree of anxiety he experiences is catastrophic, threatening to overwhelm his very existence. These children can appear to the observer to be withdrawn from their surroundings, attuned exclusively to their own inner worlds; they shun other people, ignoring, avoiding them as though they threaten danger, pain, and even annihilation.

Exploration for these children may consist of discovering the touch and sound of their own body and its parts, at an age beyond when such explorations are commonplace. Alternatively, concrete sensory experience with inanimate objects or parts of objects may become the focus of their attention. Other children may evoke their curiosity and be imitated or observed from a distance. Social interaction is fleeting and is often rigidly repetitive. Relating to others lacks the spontaneity, warmth, and the joy of human companionship. These children's deficits in communication may be compounded by affective expression that is primitive and underdeveloped, often bizarre and difficult to comprehend.

The play of these very anxious children lies within the outer margins of play activity. Although it is qualitatively different from mainstream play activity, however, to the extent that the child becomes engrossed in his activity—activity that is apparently at his own initiative, an expression of his feelings, focused on himself, persons, objects, or surroundings—he is playing. Developmentally, this play activity represents an early level of play, play activity that is not yet represented using consensual symbols or communicated through the reciprocal use of language.

What sorts of children present with very anxious play activity? Although some children present with all of their play activity at this very anxious level, other children experience encapsulated moments of regression when their play activity presents with these characteristics. Generally speaking, children within the autistic spectrum of disorders are most likely to play exclusively in this extremely anxious/isolated manner.

Three severe deficits that impact on the development of play activity distinguish autistic children from other retarded and psychiatric groups (Chicchetti, Beeghly, & Weiss-Perry 1994). These deficiencies occur in the areas of symbolic play, communication, language, and social interaction (Baron-Cohen 1989; Hobson 1986; Rutter & Garmezy 1983; Sigman & Mundy 1987). In autistic children, all these weaknesses combine in what has been characterized as a *generalized social–cognitive deficit* (Dawson 1989; Rutter 1978, 1983). Many autistic-spectrum children never develop language or symbolic play. In those children that do, symbolic play is most often rigid, repetitive, and stereotyped, lacking the varying degrees of complexity, fluidity, and creativity observed in normal, character- disordered, and mentally retarded children.

In her study of children who had experienced neglect, abuse, and severe disturbances in their relationships with caregivers, Selma Fraiberg (1982) described defensive behaviors that could be observed in early infancy (birth to 18 months). Since these behaviors appeared in a preverbal period, prior to the development of evocative memory, they were not yet expressive of internal conflicts between drives and an emerging ego organization. Rather, they appeared as symptomatic behaviors in very young children who had suffered environmental and relationship deficiencies. For other children, the same type of defenses might arise from neurological or constitutional issues or a combination of etiologic factors.

Selma Fraiberg and her colleagues observed these patterns of defensive behaviors between mother and child during home visits. The pathological behaviors included total or near-total avoidance of the mother by the child; freezing in an almost complete immobilization of posture, motility, or articulation; and fighting in an effort to ward off feelings of extreme helplessness and dissolution of self. Two of these defensive behaviors—avoidance and freezing—are included in our cluster of very anxious/isolated play behaviors; identification with the aggressor (fighting) is classified in the cluster of polarized/rigid defensive–coping strategies.

Frances Tustin (1990) has described autistic impediments to the development of play activity. Among the children she observed some exhibited these impediments from birth, while others seemed to be reacting to extreme deprivation. She described these children as compensating for early psychological deficiencies by overvaluing tactile physical contacts and the sensations they aroused; only what was tangible and physically present was felt to exist. The overwhelming influence of the immediate present led to a diminution or near extinction of memories and images, blocking imagination essential for the development of play activity. The autistic child's preoccupation with sensory objects protected him from experiencing loss, thereby precluding the use of images and memory to recall persons and objects.

The very anxious/isolated player demonstrates this reliance for security upon immediate sensorimotor experience. At this level of playing, the child is not differentiating clearly between self and other, between what is internal and what is external. Rather, he is playing out a muted state of consciousness, in which he clings to toys, seems oblivious to pain or pleasure, and destroys the world as we know it in order to hold on to his protective inner subjective state.

This state of "nothingness" and its inhibiting effect on play activity is illustrated by the case of four-year-old Jane described by Tustin (1990). Jane was observed in her play group, where she stood at the edge of the group, eyeing the other children while clutching a dome-shaped shell in her hand. She was afraid of making contact with the other children and would look longingly at them. She was very constricted in her choice of play materials and would purposely choose defective ones, such as broken pencils that she would try to draw with. She often used the word "nothing" in her conversation. For example, she drew "snakes doing nothing," and she also drew something she called "nothing going very fast." After talking about a loaf of bread that had been ruined by the rain, Jane drew "spots of nothing."

Tustin observed Jane using the shell compulsively to fill a void; having said "nothing" she would take a peep at her shell. Used in this manner, the shell functioned as a sensation object to compensate for Jane's feeling of "nothingness." By clinging to the shell, Jane also clung to a feeling of existence; the shell shielded her from the terror of feeling she had lost a vital part of her body and reassured her that she would continue to "go-on-being." At the same time, the shell did not exist symbolically and could not be used in that way (Milner 1955). Thus, the shell could not be represented in memory or used as a touchstone for fantasy to further the development of play activity. The shell as object could not be redefined or modified; it remained adhered to the immediate present. Any effort to modify the function of the shell in any way would be resisted by the child at all costs.

Donald Meltzer (1975) and his colleagues reported on a number of autistic children who had been treated with psychoanalysis. Meltzer described dismantling as a defensive process of eradicating meaning from an experience by diminishing it to a level where it no longer can be comprehended as common sense. Reducing an activity to this level eradicates emotional significance and symbolic form. The event is not contained and is observed to be only disparate pieces, various parts that exist in a random, mechanical way. The child uses dismantling to reduce an experience to parts devoid of meaning. If the event is not represented symbolically, it is unavailable to inner thought processes and cannot be retained in memory through representation.

Meltzer reflected how a mental process, such as dismantling, at first used defensively can also potentially be used by the child for the purpose of adaptation. He outlined how the child can begin to create an experience of inner and outer (see Bick 1968 who describes this process as the creation of an emotional skin) that progressively expands to become a four-dimensional emotional space (inside me, outside me, inside you, outside you). Attainment of the level of development depends upon the existence of a relationship that affords the child an opportunity to contain his emotional experience and give it meaning. Play activity is the medium that provides the child with opportunities for this development of self. Once meaning is achieved, the reverse dissolution of a whole into its parts (dismantling) can be experienced as a creative abstraction, rather than an act of destruction. Thus, it is the clinician's capacity to recognize and contain the child's emotional states in a state of playfulness that promotes the growth of mind within the child. This "holding function" (Bion 1962) of the therapist gives form to the inchoate pieces and encourages the emergence of patterning within the child's emotional experience. Meltzer's comments highlight the interface between coping and defensive functions, with the balance contingent upon the subjective experience of the child. The spectrum of four clusters of play strategies allows for observation of this movement (or fluctuation) within subjective experience while the child is playing.

Defensive–Coping Strategies Used By the Extremely Anxious/Isolated Child

Using the CPTI the observer obtains a complete measure of extreme anxiety and of the various ways in which it affects the child's capacity to play. It enables the therapist to document the presence versus absence of play activity; the presence or absence of symbolic play activity, the relative levels of cognitive representations used in the play activity, the distinctive patterns of feelings expressed in the play activity, the varying levels of social and verbal communication within the play activity, and finally the coping/defensive strategies observed within the play activity.

The manual of the CPTI (Kernberg, Chazan & Normandin 1997) defines nine strategies in the cluster of extremely anxious/isolated play activities. In addition to Selma Fraiberg, Frances Tustin, and Donald Meltzer, several other child theorists have described the use of these strategies and their impact on the playing child (Beebe & Stern 1977; Klein 1930; Mahler 1972a, 1972b; Sander 1983; Ogden 1989). Their work also contributed to the definitions of extremely anxious/isolated play strategies compiled in the CPTI manual and listed below.

Dedifferentiation

Several different items lose their separate identity and become homogeneous. Order is removed from an organization, so that it is rendered chaotic.

"Everything is mixed together; these are all the same."

Constriction

There is an extremely persistent, perseverative, rigid repetition of thoughts, affect, and behavior. All three characteristics must be present. Constriction involves a significant narrowing of the self or the child's perception of the other.

> "It must stay in one area; it must be limited to the same story, with the same beginning and ending."

De-animation

An animate object is rendered lifeless.

> "It is still, not doing anything."

Dispersal

Dangerous aspects of the self or other are broken into fragments and scattered. Note: The object may be disparate pieces (such as Lego); the whole object need not be formed concretely in order to be scattered.

> "It is broken into pieces and spread around so it will not be dangerous anymore."

Dismantling

A person or toy is reduced to disconnected segments.

> "It is disconnected, the parts (of the body, of a theme) are no longer bound to each other."

Autistic Encapsulation

Through the play activity the child communicates an insulation of self from his surroundings and his therapist. The play activity is an all-encompassing, protective barrier.

> "I am keeping it walled inside."

Fusion

Boundaries between self and other, between internal and external worlds, are blurred into a state of continuous oneness.

> "I get (it gets) lost in a boundlessness with everything. Everything is all mixed together."

Freezing

The functioning of the self/other person is halted for the purpose of survival.

"To control my terror I make everything stop and stand still."

Hypochondriasis

A dangerous feeling or impulse is experienced as residing within a particular body organ. This part of the body is perceived as being capable of destroying the individual. Instead of terror being felt because of others, the feeling is transformed into a terror of part of the self, experienced as pain in part of the body.

"The terror is taken in again and hurts me."

Reversal of Affect

The appropriate feeling is replaced by its opposite, often a bizarre and inappropriate opposite.

"I am terrified, it makes me laugh; it is hilarious!"

Clinical Case: A Child Called Sammy

At the time of referral, the aspect of Sammy's difficulties that caused his parents most grief was the fact that he could not play. Twenty-eight months old, he was trapped within a rigid, at times terrifying, isolated world. He was incapable of solving the simplest problem, experienced intense, constricted feelings, and could communicate only pain and discomfort through his high-pitched, shrill cry.

At 26 months of age Sammy had been given the diagnosis pervasive developmental disorder with autistic features by the diagnostic team in his local school district and by several independent consultants. Sammy's parents were shocked and overwhelmed by this diagnosis. Meeting with Sammy's parents brought an important reminder that any diagnostic formulation for the child is also a critical intervention for the parents.

The behaviors Sammy exhibited included significant receptive and expressive language delays, delayed play skills, withdrawn and bizarre social interaction, hyperactivity, and a short attention span. He was motorically driven and had virtually no frustration tolerance; his mother felt she could not connect with him in a "normal" way. Both parents viewed Sammy as an oddball and laughed nervously when they described him, a response that seemed a defense against feelings of helplessness.

Sammy was the younger son of Mr and Mrs M. The firstborn, Michael, was 20 months older, an alert, highly verbal child whose play skills were advanced. Michael occasionally experienced mild fears. The parents were both skilled professionals, but Mrs M. had chosen to be a full-time homemaker, having decided to leave an excellent position seven months earlier. Mrs M. had returned to work when Sammy was eight months old and continued working until he was 21 months old. It was when she stopped working that Mrs M. became aware of Sammy's troubled development and began to seek assistance.

Sammy was conceived when his older brother was 11 months old. The pregnancy was uncomplicated. There were concerns regarding insufficient weight gain, but five routine sonograms revealed a normal embryonic course. Delivery was spontaneous; birthweight was seven pounds. Breast-feeding was attempted for one month but could not be established successfully. Mrs M. was deeply hurt and disappointed by Sammy's rejection of breast-feeding. For the first three months, Sammy was generally unfocused and seemed to be uncomfortable or unhappy most of the time.

Sammy's parents both reported that it was difficult to read Sammy's signals and to understand what he wanted. It was also difficult to elicit smiles or laughter. Motor milestones were within normal limits; in contrast, language development was significantly delayed. Sammy said single words at between 14 and 15 months and two-word phrases at two years. Audiology evaluation at two years was normal. Most importantly, Sammy's parents were concerned that he was "not attached enough." During his first year of life, he pushed both parents away and became attached to a plush dog. At one year he became attached to his father and a warm, caring housekeeper. Sammy first began to show affection for his mother at 18 months. His brother, Michael, was always someone Sammy sought out. In addition to his plush dog, Sammy clung to a baseball bat and a hammer, objects he used for hitting, and his bottle, which he wanted to dangle from his mouth at all times.

The Early Phase of Treatment

Although Sammy's parents described Sammy as being unable to play, when I first met him it was clear that this statement was not an accurate assessment of their son's capacities. It was not that Sammy did not play, but that he played in a manner unrecognizable as such to either of his parents. Although Sammy was playing, he was playing differently from other children his age, and in a manner highly idiosyncratic to Sammy. He grasped his two sensory objects at all times, hard (hammer in hand) and soft (bottle dangling from teeth). These objects were not play objects per se; rather, they were viewed by Sammy as an extension of his own body. Any effort to remove them from his grasp resulted in a shrill, piercing cry of protest. It took all of Sammy's parents' energies to calm him and their attention was focused on supplying and retrieving these objects. Thus, their attention was diverted from what Sammy would do once he had the objects in tow. In fact, he would explore his surroundings for sporadic bits of time and engage objects briefly, knocking his body against others and then returning to his parent. Just as he played in an idiosyncratic fashion, his attempts to engage his parents' attention were unfocused and diffuse (for example, nudging them, continuously wailing, and wandering aimlessly about).

My earliest glimpses of Sammy's capacity for play occurred at our second meeting, when he arrived in the company of his older brother. He in fact did succeed in locating a truck and wheeling it along the edge of the table, all the time eyeing his older brother. At the moment his older brother picked up a toy, Sammy made a beeline for that toy. He physically attacked his brother, tried to grab the toy, and could not be placated. The older brother relinquished the toy, and Sammy proceeded to play with it briefly and then ran back to connect with mother (all the time he held both sensory objects in tow). In this session, Sammy demonstrated that he could play, but he was also continually distracted by trying to control his surround. His mother was unable to engage him in play, as she was always navigating a path of survival in the field of battle.

In these early meetings Sammy demonstrated an acute awareness of his sensory environment and of minute changes in his surroundings. He was capable of diffusing his attention, so that it scattered and wandered from object to object without sustaining focus on himself or the other person.

He carried his "autistic sensation objects" (hammer, baseball bat) with him in an effort to feel hard and strong. For Sammy these hard sensations were experienced through the activity of banging. In sessions Sammy was observed to bang with his head, his arms, or his whole torso, as he would bang with his hard objects. According to Tustin, these hard objects help the child to feel safe; they are the hard part of himself, a barrier to protect him from the dangerous "not me" objects that threaten him and his existence.

Sammy also demonstrated the use of what Tustin refers to as "autistic sensation shapes." These arise from soft bodily sensations, such as the flow of urine from the body, bubbles of spit from the mouth, diarrhea, or vomit. They can also be engendered by holding an outside object loosely or pressing gently against it, by rocking or spinning, and by hand and body stereotypic movements. The shapes thus engendered are felt by the child to have no separateness from his own body, nor are they related to the shape of any particular objects. Like autistic objects they are idiosyncratic to the individual child. They are "tactile hallucinations," and because they are soothing and calming, they are a bodily form of tranquilizer. Sammy's soft shapes included his saliva, produced by voluntary bubbling, sucking, and drooling; his bottle; his plush dog; and the soft contours of his mother's body.

The method of intervention chosen for Sammy and his family was simultaneous treatment. In simultaneous treatment the parent and child are treated by the same therapist. The focus of treatment is on the parent–child relationship and on the separate as well as shared subjective experience of parent and child. Thus, the therapist is concerned not only with the interactions between parent and child but also with the individual representational experience of both. Since Sammy was a young child, the child sessions would be dyadic meetings, with both parent and child present. Mrs M. was receptive to the suggestion that she and Sammy meet jointly with the therapist twice a week. At times, Sammy's brother Michael would be present as well. In addition Mrs M. would have her own individual sessions with the therapist on a weekly basis. Because Mr M. was continuing twice-weekly analytic treatment, contact with him would consist of monthly parent meetings focusing on issues of parent management.

With parental consent, all joint mother–child sessions were videotaped. Analyses of Sammy's play activity were based on ratings of these video-taped sessions using the CPTI. A detailed description of the complete course of Sammy's treatment has been published previously (Chazan 1995).

SEGMENTATION OF THE SESSION

In what follows, the sequence of segments within the session is described consecutively. Each successive segment is identified as pre-play, play activity, non-play, or interruption. The duration of the segment (minutes:seconds) is indicated in parentheses.

> Sammy enters the session crying inconsolably for his bottle. He runs to the door, bangs on it, and cannot be soothed (non-play, 1:44). Sammy and his mother leave the room to retrieve the bottle (interruption, 0:49). Sammy and his mother return and she sits him on her lap and gives him the bottle. He takes the bottle in his hands and drinks (non-play, 0:58). The therapist takes out some rhythm instruments and begins to play the triangle. Sammy watches the therapist, interested in what she is doing (pre-play, 1:33). Sammy leaves his mother's lap, and with bottle dangling from his mouth he begins to play the triangle (play activity, 0:52). Sammy returns to cuddle with mother (non-play, 1:00). Sammy comes back to play the triangle again, while the therapist sings (play activity, 1:49). Sammy watches while the therapist plays a drum (pre-play, 1:41). Sammy sits on the floor sucking his bottle, he lifts the bottle to *reference his mother's face*. She smiles back at him and hugs him (non-play, 2:17). Sammy remains seated on the floor with the therapist. He begins to play with a sorting toy, putting different shapes into a container that then makes a sound (play activity, 4:16). Sammy returns to sit on his mother's lap and begins to suck on his bottle, which has been dangling from his mouth (non-play, 3:01). Sammy gets down from his mother's lap and joins the therapist at the dollhouse (pre-play, 0:34). Sammy walks away from the therapist and begins to wander about. His mother moves from the couch and gives him a hug (non-play, 3:35). Sammy communicates that he wants the "choo-choo" put together. Bottle dangling from his mouth he engages therapist and mother in play (play activity, 5:52). (This was the longest play activity segment and the one rated. A detailed narrative of this segment follows segmentation of the entire session.) Sammy walks away from the activity and gives his bottle to his mother (non-play,

0:48). Sammy walks back to the trains and looks at the setup (pre-play, 1:55). Sammy wanders away and climbs up to the table to play with a puzzle (play activity, 4:26). Sammy walks away and wanders around the room, and his mother holds him (non-play, 5:06). Sammy wanders over to the triangle and begins to play with the therapist's assistance (play activity, 4:22). The therapist ended the session.

In this first session rated, Sammy and his mother were alone with the therapist. She was less detached from Sammy and responded warmly to his overtures: the mother's depression had clearly diminished. The therapist was active in initiating communication between mother and child. Sammy used the soft sensation object, his bottle, to initiate contact with his mother. For example, while engaged with the therapist Sammy paused and raised his bottle in the direction of his mother, and a long moment of mutual gaze (a first) ensued. This visual focus, or holding, became an important medium for the growth of the parent–child relationship. Once visual contact was established, Sammy could begin to seek contact with his mother more directly.

Segmentation of the therapy session revealed that 45 percent of this session was spent in play activity. The strong alliance between therapist and child worked toward enabling Sammy's mother to observe his potential for playfulness, which had been hidden by a veil of nonrelatedness. Pre-play activity constituted 12 percent of the session and consisted mainly of Sammy's response to the therapist's invitation to play. Non-play activity accounted for 40 percent of the session and consisted of interactions between mother and child, as well as Sammy's aimless wandering around the room. There was one brief interruption as mother and Sammy departed to retrieve his bottle. Without the bottle it would not have been possible to calm, engage, or focus Sammy. He did, however, relinquish the bottle to mother toward the end of the session.

DESCRIPTIVE ANALYSIS OF THE PLAY ACTIVITY SEGMENT

The following narrative of the longest play activity segment, the segment used in rating Sammy's play activity, is based upon observations of the videotaped session.

Sammy initiated play activity with a request (communicated through gesture) to put the "choo-choo" together. Mother began assisting in joining the train tracks. Sammy wandered off and then returned to the play. His bottle was in his mouth, dangling from his teeth, he held a hammer in his hand, his affect was flat. Sammy's mother was involved in the activity and was watching her child closely. Sammy asked for "track" and gestured towards the trains. His affect continued to be flat and his face non-expressive. The therapist responded: "Yes, I will get the tracks." Sammy echoed "track", all the while holding his bottle in his mouth.

The therapist asked Sammy's mother how to fit the tracks together and she started putting tracks together. The therapist asked Sammy if he would like to put tracks together. He put two train cars together. The therapist described the cars as "together." Sammy's mother constructed a setup of the tracks in a circle. Sammy put a train on the tracks; his mother watched and complimented him. He then opened and shut the door to the room very briefly; he wanted to go to the car (less than 20 seconds, insufficient time to be an interruption). Sammy went over to the dollhouse and opened and shut the windows and doors. The therapist and Sammy's mother joined him at the dollhouse. The therapist described what was happening; Sammy's mother watched. Sammy put a toy figure inside the house, then, opened and closed the windows and door. With his hammer in his hand and his bottle in his mouth Sammy wandered away from the dollhouse and joined his mother on the couch. His affect was flat; he seemed to lack energy and was fatigued.

Sammy's play activity included exploration of the room and manipulation of various toys. He also began to construct a train joining two cars together. Sammy initiated the play by indicating an interest in the trains. Both mother and therapist facilitated the play considerably by following through on Sammy's initiatives and making further suggestions. Sammy's mother initiated the setup of tracks. Sammy inhibited the play activity by leaving the room and ended the play activity by transitioning to non-play without clear evidence of satiation. He wandered away, lost focus, and went to sit on his mother's lap. It seemed as though he was tired out by the activity, but not necessarily satisfied by it, he simply could not sustain interest any longer.

STRUCTURAL ANALYSIS OF THE PLAY ACTIVITY SEGMENT

Affective Components

Sammy's emotional tone was generally sober. His face was usually non-expressive and the spectrum of affects narrow. He seemed most often to be aloof from social interaction. He expressed some curiosity about the tracks and the dollhouse, but anxiety (reflected in his wanderings) and sadness balanced the minimal pleasure from playing. His regulation of feeling states was moderate, with a bland nondescript, muted quality; transitions from one feeling state to another were always abrupt, with a swift shift from aversive to positive feelings. His emotional reactions were always appropriate to the content of the play. Sammy's attitude towards the therapist was neutral; the therapist's attitude towards Sammy was very positive.

Cognitive Components

Sammy's play activity consisted primarily of sensory and motor explorations and manipulations. He did demonstrate some understanding of "open and shut," in trying to open the door of the office and the windows and doors of the dollhouse. He put a small boy figure inside the house, an early precursor of role-play. He also understood the action of connecting the railroad tracks as the joining of two separate pieces.

Narrative Components

Although there was no continuous narrative to the play activity the topics of the play included the train tracks and the house. Themes were sparsely organized around the activities of joining and separating (the tracks), coming and going (the toy train and the office door), and opening and shutting (dollhouse door and windows). Sammy was silent most of the time. He verbalized "track" to refer to the railroad track. The therapist and Mrs M. usually gave verbal descriptions of what they were doing in the play, for example putting the cars of the train "together"; they were occasionally silent, and at times they imitated sounds of the train. They both also verbally reflected upon Sammy's actions in a supportive manner.

Developmental Components

Sammy's play activity was somewhat immature for his chronological age. He did not engage in elaborated symbolic play and gave only a hint of the play potential that might emerge over time. His interest in vehicles reflected primarily a masculine orientation; however, again the evidence was scarce and minimally suggestive of gender preference. Sammy played alone most of the time, but he was aware of the presence of the therapist and his mother, who made efforts to make their presence important to Sammy's play. There was some evidence of parallel play activity as Sammy played at joining the tracks alongside the therapist and his mother, who were similarly engaged in putting together the railroad tracks.

FUNCTIONAL ANALYSIS OF THE PLAY ACTIVITY SEGMENT

In his play activity Sammy demonstrated some minimal attempts at *problem-solving*, an adaptive coping strategy, in attempting to put the railroad tracks together. He also evidenced minimal *avoidance* of interaction with the adults and *regression*, suggesting some evidence of conflict. There was no evidence of rigid/polarized defenses. Most prominent were strategies reflecting extreme anxiety and isolation. These strategies included *dismantling* and *constriction*. Constriction was seen in the narrow band of play interests observed and the lack of variation in play activity. Dismantling was observed as a more extreme manifestation of avoidance, where Sammy wandered around the room aimlessly, seemingly unaware and unresponsive to human interaction. When addressed at these times, he would not turn away; he would simply respond as if the person addressing him did not exist. It was necessary to confront him firmly and touch him to reestablish contact. Sammy seemed to have little vitality or energy to invest in relatedness, and he would spin off by himself to recoup. A promising aspect of this play activity segment was Sammy's mother's close involvement with the play, as active observer, commentator, and player. Also promising was Sammy's return to her, joining her on the couch as the play segment ended. Sammy was unaware of himself as playing during this play activity segment, but his mother showed first signs of being aware of her own enjoyment in being an active player.

The complex duet between Sammy and his mother continued to unfold in treatment, with visual seeking and physical contact becoming important parameters in the growing secure attachment between mother and child. In intervening sessions Mrs M. began to invite Sammy to games of "Finding Mommy," when she would hide under a hat, and "Finding Mommy Ghost," when she was hidden under a table. Sammy began to engage his mother by playing he was a kitten. At first it was difficult to discern the direction the role playing would take. Would Sammy *become* the little kitten that Mommy adored? No, *Sammy decided he was Sammy*, playing at being a kitten, and in this play activity he discovered a new sense of his identity.

In a following session, another meaningful moment occurred when Sammy was hard at work and absorbed in playing with his sand toys. For 15 minutes Sammy was engrossed in covering and uncovering a dump truck. Mother was involved in an active way only minimally; she sat nearby making accompanying noises of a truck digging. The climax of the play activity came when Sammy held up the sand tray and with a broad smile announced that he was "Done." Ending the play activity segment with satiation indicated Sammy had achieved a conceptualization of beginning, middle, and end and was beginning to comprehend the constancy of objects over time. These observations highlighted the important role of play in forming and strengthening secure bonds between parent and child (Chazan 1995). The gains were made indirectly through metaphor, but the reference was a direct one to the parent–child relationship.

A Session Nine Months Later

SEGMENTATION OF THE SESSION

In this later session there were 14 segments, as compared with 20 segments in the earlier session. As in the discussion of the earlier session, the succession of segments is reviewed and the longest play activity segment is subjected to structural and functional analysis.

Sammy enters the office, sits down on the couch, and asks to see the therapist's dog (non-play, 1:15). When his request is denied, he gets off the couch and meows, playing he is a cat. His mother comments, "The pussycat's here." Sammy plays with a box on the floor (play activity, 2:33). Sammy begins to talk again about wanting to see the dog, gesturing towards the door of the office (non-play, 2:33). Sammy leaves the office to see the dog with the therapist. The therapist brings her dog momentarily into the waiting room to greet Sammy (interruption, 2:56). Sammy returns to the office and sits down to eat his snack, a regular feature of our sessions (non-play, 1:29). As he is eating, mother and Sammy begin to play with a globe on the table. They play briefly at going and coming from different parts of the world (play activity, 0:52). Sammy returns to eating (non-play, 0:53). Sammy begins to play at feeding a toy turtle and then at feeding his mother (play activity, 2:41). Sammy gets up and takes out a toy truck preparatory to playing (pre-play, 1:19). Sammy begins putting together train tracks. As he puts the train on the track, he says "Bye-bye" and pushes the train around the tracks (play activity, 6:54). There is a pause in the play activity. Sammy looks up gazing lovingly at his mother. His mother returns his gaze warmly (non-play, 0:33). Sammy whispers to his mother secretly about the truck. They seem to be plotting together (pre-play, 0:55). Sammy looks at the therapist and smiles. He says "big truck" and pushes the truck out from under a chair toward the train tracks. This is the longest play activity segment of the session (play activity, 15:00). It is significant that this long activity segment is continuous with the previous play activity segment involving pushing the train around the track. It is Sammy's idea to bring the truck and train together to tell his story. The therapist initiates cleaning up that ends the session (non-play, 2:17).

COMPARISON OF SEGMENTATION OF TWO SESSIONS

In session two Sammy increased the time he spent in play activity from 45 to 66 percent (see Figure 5.1). Clearly Sammy was able to play early in treatment, given the increased focus of his mother and the support of the therapist. The percentage of time spent in non-play decreased from 40 to 21 percent from session one to session two. In session two it seemed that Sammy could not refrain from playing; even while eating he began to interact playfully with his mother. Playfulness had clearly become his major way of being with the therapist and his mother during sessions. Pre-play decreased from 12 to 5 percent from session one to two, reflecting greater spontaneity and liveliness in Sammy's play. Interruptions occurred in both sessions at the beginning of the session. Both of these interruptions were instances of Sammy's asserting his will to do something specific before beginning the session.

Excerpt From the Later Session

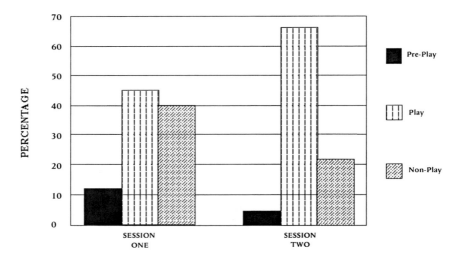

Figure 5.1 Changes in Segmentation in the Course of Sammy's Treatment

This play activity segment was a continuation of an earlier play activity segment in which Sammy and his mother were coupling tracks together. It began when Sammy started to roll a large truck out from under a chair toward the train tracks. He was very animated and excited by the crash of the truck with the tracks.

Mother:	The truck is on the track. Stop the train!
Sammy:	Uh-oh! *(Babytalk)*
Mother:	Shall we try again?

(Sammy's mother helps him to recouple the train. Sammy continues playing with the train for a long while; then it comes apart)

Sammy:	Stop the train!

Therapist:	*(On play phone)* Hello, train company, is the train coming on time? It's late!
Sammy:	It broke.
Therapist:	Stop! There's a truck on the track.
Sammy:	Stop! Back up! *(Sammy picks up play phone and speaks animatedly in babytalk)*
Mother:	There's a truck on the track. We need a tow truck to bring it off.

(Sammy and his mother, after extended combined effort, manage to tow the truck off the track)

Therapist:	Is the train on time?

(Sammy puts the breakdown car back on the track)

Sammy:	Oh, no!

(Sammy and his mother confer together. The therapist speaks on the toy phone. Sammy puts train cars together. Finally the breakdown car clears the track and the truck goes on its way)

Sammy:	*(With little fireman figure and fire truck)* Hurry! Come and fix the track! There's a fire on the track!

(The toy fireman walks up the ladder. Sammy continues to play at being the toy fireman going up and down the ladder. The therapist helps Sammy to put the toy fire engine together. Animated conversation (not understandable) between child and therapist is accompanied by much excitement. Sammy finally pushes the train around the track, while he continues to talk without stopping (not understandable). Sammy takes the toy fireman off the track and the fire is out)

The therapist initiated cleaning up the toys, as it was time for the session to end.

DESCRIPTIVE ANALYSIS OF THE PLAY ACTIVITY SEGMENT

Sammy's play activity during this play activity segment was categorized as exploratory, manipulative, and construction play. In addition, the play activity was a literal duplication of events in the everyday world, where vehicles get stuck on railroad tracks and need to be hauled away and then the tracks have to be repaired. The story was action-oriented and realistic; it could also be understood as a metaphor. The truck crashing with the train was Sammy's depiction of trauma that impeded his connection to his family and the world around him. The train is rescued from disaster, the truck is freed to resume its journey, and the little fireman comes to repair the disconnection and fire on the tracks.

Sammy clearly initiated this play activity segment and schemed his ideas with his mother. Although he could not clearly verbalize his story, the dyad communicated through gestures and facial expression. Sammy also was active in facilitating the play. He was joined in his efforts by the facilitative activities of his mother and his therapist. There was no inhibition of the play. The play activity was ended solely at the suggestion of the therapist. In this session Sammy took a definite role of leadership in planning, framing, and sustaining the play activity.

STRUCTURAL ANALYSIS OF THE PLAY ACTIVITY SEGMENT

Affective Components

The affective ratings revealed a significant shift in Sammy's affective expression between sessions. The most significant shifts, as anticipated, were toward significantly greater pleasure, a widening of spectrum of affects, more flexibility in modulation, smoother transitions, and more positive tone toward the therapist. While there was a diminution in aloofness and sadness, there was an increase in anxiety and worry.

Cognitive Components

The cognitive ratings indicated a shift from precursors of role-play in session one to more advanced individual (as toy fireman) and dyadic role-play (talking on phone to therapist as conductor of the train), with some suggestion of triadic role-play (mother, therapist, and Sammy as fixers of the track), in session two. All representations of objects and persons remained stable. The style of representation of objects and persons was consistently realistic. The toy objects were also used realistically (a toy track was used as a track).

Narrative Components

There was continuity in topic around transportation and home in both sessions that expanded in the second session to become a train with track obstruction and subsequently a fire on the track. The theme of the play progressed from separation and connectedness to reconstruction and overcoming mechanical problems. Once Sammy was able to complete the construction of a setup of tracks, he introduced issues of blockage and possible destruction. Each one of these obstacles was solved in turn, with Sammy emerging victorious as the train continued its journey.

The language subscales reflected a shift in the use of silence as well as of words. In the first session, Sammy was predominantly silent; in the second session, silence was more typical of the therapist. In the second session, Sammy demonstrated imitation of sounds, verbalization of a single role, and talk within the metaphor. The therapist in the second session paralleled Sammy's verbalization of a single role and speech within the metaphor.

Developmental Components

Developmental ratings revealed an increment to age-appropriate play activity in the second session. Gender identity of the play was predominantly masculine. The most significant finding occurred in the social level of the play activity. Sammy made significant gains in social level of play, progressing from solitary (aware) to reciprocal play activity (give and take with his mother and the therapist).

FUNCTIONAL ANALYSIS OF THE PLAY ACTIVITY SEGMENT

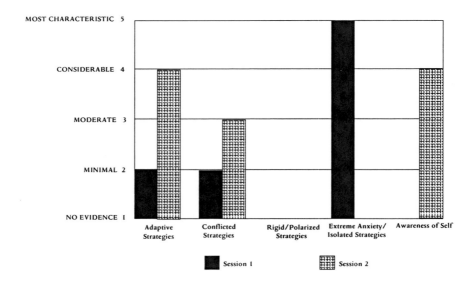

Figure 5.2 Sammy's Coping–Defensive Strategies in the Course of Treatment

Figure 5.2 illustrates the changes that occurred over time in the functional analysis of Sammy's play activity. In the second session, Sammy demonstrated considerable use of adaptive coping strategies in his play, including *anticipation, sublimation, affiliation,* and *altruism.* He was fully engaged in collaboration with his mother and therapist in the play *(affiliation)*; he anticipated the need to stop the toy train and call for assistance *(anticipation).* Sammy's affective involvement in the play indicated the presence of *sublimation,* a strategy capable of converting anxiety-evoking circumstances into constructive, creative activity. Sammy's concern with disruption to the train's progress barely concealed his anxiety and worry about cars crashing and breaking down. His solution to this crisis was to reach out to others (communicate by phone) in order to seek repair. Thanks to the *altruistic* efforts of the toy fireman the train could continue its journey.

Conflicted play strategies were present in the second session to a moderate degree. Sammy used *projection* to invest the toys (train, fireman) with expressing his own needs. He used the strategy of *doing and undoing* as the toy fireman went up and down the ladder repeatedly while the fire was put out. Most remarkable was the absence of either rigid/polarized or extreme anxiety/isolated defensive strategies in the second session.

These dramatic changes in overall function of the play activity were also reflected in the summary variable awareness-of-self playing which shifted from no evidence in session one to considerable evidence in session two. Sammy clearly made large developmental strides in treatment. These gains were reflected in measurable changes in his play activity.

This videotaped case study enabled me to view and review the emergence of human connectedness based on joy and the growth of attachment through play activity. There were many reasons underlying the choice of topics and themes for the play activity. These topics and themes included movement, the transportation of people and objects, separation and return, breakdown and repair. Most importantly, the play activity dealt with togetherness, as Sammy and his mother repeatedly "coupled" train tracks and cars. The process of Sammy's growth and development was documented using the CPTI and was traced qualitatively and quantitatively through the progression of play data. One clear example of Sammy's new capacity for sharing feelings and ideas occurred in the second session. The longest play activity segment was preceded by a 20-second interval of non-play when mother and child exchanged loving glances and then conspired intimately together (pre-play), previewing the play activity to come. The togetherness of this dyad was the happiness of reunion. In the shared joy and anticipatory plans for playing, Sammy's mother encountered the child she had yearned for, as Sammy discovered he was a player.

How does one account for Sammy's striking progress? Maturity is always a potent force propelling a child forward toward growth and development. Certainly, in Sammy's case maturity was a partial answer to account for his developmental course. Controlled studies are necessary to clarify the respective roles of maturation and therapeutic intervention. It is important to note that the enhancement of Sammy's affective and cognitive development progressed at a quickened pace and with emotional changes that exceeded expectations. It seems reasonable to conclude that the therapeutic intervention of simultaneous treatment was an important component in contributing to these welcome changes.

CHAPTER 6

Play Activity, The Player, and Development of the Self

Of'times the child knows
but cannot tell in words
a truth beyond all else.
"The play's the thing!"
that's all there is
and e'er will be.

The Function of Play and Playfulness

Playing and growing are synonymous with life itself. Playfulness bespeaks creativity and action, change and the possibility of transformation. Play activity thus reflects the very existence of the self, that part of the organism that exists both independently and interdependently, that can reflect upon itself and be aware of its own existence. In being playful the child attains a degree of autonomy sustained by representations of his inner and outer worlds.

The Child's Awareness of Himself as a Player

The child's awareness that he is playing is a summary variable. It includes both the child's awareness of himself and his awareness of being in a state of play. When a child lacks awareness of himself as a player, he also lacks a capacity to be aware of the special, unique attributes of playing. The play is then experienced as immediate and real. Play activity that is experienced as real rather than pretense is placed within constraints; it lacks the flexibility and modulation of more adaptive play. An example of the difference between the real and the pretend would be the difference between a professional ball player and a child imagining to be his favorite player running all the bases in his backyard. One would be imaginary, the other a real event. The child who is closely tied to a set of concrete play behaviors is unable to create an imaginary narrative. Once the child becomes capable of using objects and persons in his play in a symbolic way, the variety of strategies used in play activity expands rapidly. As the child begins to use play activity as trial action on the path to mastery, he may attempt various maneuvers not used previously. Similarly, with awareness of the boundary of make-believe the child's imagination expands to include diverse perspectives and infinite possibilities. With each expansion of his play activity the child becomes increasingly aware of new aspects of himself.

Revisiting Carla

Carla's play activity, described in Chapter 2, revealed a shift from repetitive mocking and aggressive actions to benevolent and pleasurable activity. The significant shift in behavior toward the doll reflected a shift in Carla's attitude toward herself. At first she was rigidly repeating a pathological identification with a dangerous and assaultive parent. Then, after sharing an imaginative moment with her therapist, a transformation occurred. Carla became aware of the beauty of the falling snow contained in the paperweight. The beauty of this perception was translated into a transformation in her role toward the doll to become a caring and companionable parent. The experience of transformation in play activity enhanced Carla's awareness that as a player she could change terror of the past into a pleasurable moment in the present.

Carla also had learned that she could pretend and that pretending could heal. Perhaps she discovered this state of mind as a very young child, and that discovery enabled her to cope with the difficult circumstance of being raised by deaf-mute parents. She told her therapist that she could make music, she could wind the music box! Winding the music box was a real accomplishment. The metacommunication was that she could listen and she could hear. In the past the self-discovery of being a person who could hear was a real discovery that may have sparked imaginings about the future. Carla could begin to imagine interactions with people other than herself, empathic people who could speak and listen. These imaginings were actualized in her play therapy.

The Development of a Capacity for Pretense and Theory of Mind

The capacity to pretend precedes the capacity for symbolic thought. It is evident in the play of infants between 10 and 18 months of age (Bates, Benigni, Bretherton, Camaioni, & Votterra 1979). Jan Drucker (1979) refers to an *endowing process* that predates symbolic representation. This aspect of early experience enables the very young child to organize his world on the basis of personal understandings gleaned from earliest parent–child relationships. These very early experiences with another person endow the process of emergence of imaginings and pretense. (See also Mayes & Cohen 1992; Stern 1974, 1992.)

Pretense is also an important component in a child's acquiring the understanding that other people act from their own perspective, called the child's *theory of mind* (Wellman 1990). Around two years of age, children usually learn that people act on the basis of their desires. Around age four, children acquire the understanding that people act on the basis of their beliefs and intentions. They also begin to distinguish acts done on purpose from accidental acts. Understanding pretense as a state of mind is essential to these later developments in theory of mind, as pretense involves the ability to represent another person's mental attitude (Leslie 1987). Thus, two-year-olds can infer what another person can see, and they can put objects in and out of sight. By age three or four, children can infer how these objects appear to other persons (Flavell 1977).

On the basis of these findings, it seems probable that Carla could understand at a very young age, that her parents could not hear (an endowed understanding of deficiency, or loss). Moreover, later on she could represent herself as someone who could hear, and she could anticipate a future experience of sharing listening with someone else. This pretend experience was enacted in her play activity with her therapist. The degree of Carla's awareness of herself as a player also reflected her degree of understanding of, or empathy with, the experience of another. The transference relationship with her therapist reawakened fantasy yearnings from the past that defined herself, Carla, as a hearing and caring person in relationship to another caring and hearing person. The trigger for this shared experience was a visual one, the falling snow; it led to a verbal response by the therapist, who reflected upon what she saw with an expression of awe regarding the glittering sight.

Jerome Bruner (1990) traced an early stage in the development of theory of mind to deitic gaze. In this state, the infant spontaneously looks in the direction of another person's gaze in order to check out what that person is looking at; reading information from the person's eyes as at a later date the infant will read information from the pointing finger. Actions of giving, showing, and pointing out objects involve facial processing. The infant makes eye contact and alternates his gazing at the person with looking at the target. Later the other person's appraisal of the object being pointed out becomes important in giving information about the other's perspective (Sorce & Emde 1981). These two early visual processing activities are critical in determining the child's ability to judge other people's mental states and to recognize what they are thinking and feeling (Baron-Cohen 1989, 1991, 1995).

The link between these early cognitive developments and emotional growth is close and intimate. They may be conceptualized as simultaneous cognitive-affective events in the life of the child that precede the formation of representations. Both how a child comes to understand others and how he forms secure attachments depend upon the quality of early visual attunement and the experience of pretend play (Trevarthen 1980). Distortion of these essential playful experiences, either though deprivation or trauma, leads to psychopathology. Just as play activity is the sphere within which the child's mind and emotions originally develop, it is also the sphere within which the child's mind and emotions can find repair (Singer & Singer 1990; Sutton-Smith 1976; Vygotsky 1966).

Distinguishing Reality From Fantasy

Awareness pertains to the conscious experience of the child that he is "playing at" or "playing out" a hypothetical scenario. Sigmund Freud alluded to this awareness of a distinction between the realm of make-believe and the realm of reality in his essay on Creative Writers and Daydreaming (1908).

> The opposite of play is not what is serious but what is real. In spite of all the emotion with which he cathects his world of play, the child distinguishes it quite well from reality; and he likes to link his imagined objects and situations to the tangible and visible things of the real world. This linking is all that differentiates the child's "play" from "phantasying." (p.143)

Robert Emde and colleagues (Emde, Kubrick and Oppenheim 1997) expanded on Freud's observations, placing the emergence of imagination in shared narratives at age three years. Emde and colleagues agreed that the very young child can begin to differentiate pretense and what is not pretense quite well and that much of this early imaginative activity has an adaptive future orientation. In his discussion Freud emphasized that such activity combines a current impression that arouses a wish with an earlier experience in which the wish was fulfilled, as well as an imagined anticipated future fulfillment of the wish. For example, the toddler's game of peek-a-boo involves expectations of return that are future-oriented.

The use of narratives to preview future happenings begins even earlier in the observed duet between parent and child (Trad 1993). Thus, in communicating with her infant the mother does not exactly replicate the child's expressive response but somehow changes the inflection, tone, or length of her resonating response. The parent in making these changes is previewing the next step she expects will follow in the infant's development. She is future-oriented, looking ahead to further developments that are yet to come but are not yet apparent.

As the young child experiences the difference between what he communicates and what is returned, this difference informs him in an immediate way of another psychic reality, the paradoxical world of play activity. In this paradoxical, future-oriented realm, the immediate present is replicated with something extra; the experience is never repeated in exactly the same way. This difference allows for the creation of other realms that exist as wishes, anticipations, expectations, imaginings, plays, and games that are not real and yet might, or might not, become real. As measured by the CPTI, the awareness of the child that he is playing implicitly reflects an understanding of this paradox; that thoughts and feelings can be unreal and yet imagined to be real, or possibly real, while in the state of mind of playing. The child demonstrates his acceptance of paradox (the suspension of disbelief) to the degree he seems aware of himself as a player (an imaginer) engaged in play activity.

Coping/Defensive Strategies and the Child's Emerging Sense of Self

In Chapters 2 through 5, profiles of coping/defensive strategies characteristic of different kinds of players were discussed in detail. Profiles of coping/defensive strategies were used to demonstrate progress in treatment. In addition to their use as broad measures of change in play strategies over time, these profiles can be analyzed to identify specific strengths and weaknesses in the components that comprise play activity (affective, cognitive, narrative, and developmental). It is then possible to observe how these differences affect the overall development of the child, his perceptions of his surroundings, and his emergence of a sense of self. To illustrate this kind of analysis, the cases of George (from Chapter 3) and Sammy (from Chapter 5) will be revisited in the pages to follow. It is important to recall that each coping/defensive strategy condenses several meanings. Each strategy contains an element of wish fulfillment, an element of cognitive-affective expression, and an element of interrelatedness (object relations). In revisiting George and Sammy, these separate elements will be identified, adding to the understanding of the function of the play strategies in the total development of the child.

Revisiting George

George's initial profile included defensive–coping strategies from each of the four clusters. His major conflicts centered about the expression of aggression and, on a more fundamental level, reflected insecure attachment to his parents. His relationships at home were marked by tension that started in infancy and continued with intermittent lack of social support for the family. Help from extended family or a social network might have acted as a buffer shielding George from the hostile, rejecting feelings of his parents. Instead his bonds with his parents were weakened by frequent moves and paternal absence. His sister's birth further diminished George's sense of security as he struggled to deal with his intense feelings of sibling rivalry.

At the beginning of treatment, George was clearly and consistently aware of his role as player and seemed to enjoy playing. However, he was not fully aware of the meaning of his nonverbal actions in play that at times amplified his verbalizations, and at times he gave hidden expression to his deepest longings for connection and bonding.

George's initial profile demonstrated his capacity for affiliation with the therapist and his enjoyment of problem-solving. These capacities were realized in rich fantasies in which he used his abilities to devise various possible alternatives to dilemmas. George was able to use avoidance and reaction formation to disguise threatening impulses. His play fantasies made abundant use of projection as in the use of the markers as a magical vehicle and the creation of the planet "Za" and regression to earlier levels of expression. However, George resorted to even more potent defensive strategies to achieve the control he needed. In his narrative he endowed himself with supernatural powers and rescued himself as the planet exploded using the strategies of omnipotent control: idealization. Although our hero escaped in time, there was the hint of an idealized loss that could not be restored.

Through his actions of scattering and disorganizing play materials, as well as the explosion of the imaginary planet, George conveyed his greatest fear: of losing his sense of self. He could no longer protect the earlier safe haven; he needed to separate from this earlier habitat. It took great strength to escape safely; however, there was also aggression against this earlier representation of the self that shattered violently. Although George's skills as a player were considerable, the pain he experienced was urgent, threatening to disrupt the continuity of the play through disorganization. Dispersal of play materials was the mode George used to express underlying subjective states of fragmentation in his ongoing experience of continuity of self. Thus, the planet's explosion was safely couched in play activity, while the threat to continuity in play activity occurred through the breakthrough of disorganizing aggressive impulses.

Midway through treatment, George manifested a growing bond to his therapist, reflected in affiliation and identification. He was able to use a wide variety of play materials and made frequent use of humor. Important to note is that this humor was based not only on an expression of his anxieties but also on an understanding of how these anxieties appeared from the perspective of a different "lens"—diminished and incongruous. Use of humor was the first indication of George's emergent capacity to reflect upon his feelings from a different viewpoint. This growth in cognitive flexibility seen in his social referencing was a major adaptive gain for him. Feeling more secure in his subjective experience, George was able to experiment with emotional closeness as he peered into the eye of the watching camera, detecting the thoughts and feelings of another. When the therapist asked what would happen next, he responded with positive anticipation as he began to enlarge upon his play narrative. These growing feelings of secure attachment formed the foundation for continuing progress through play activity.

Trusting the therapist, George began to approach the camera lens playfully, conveying his hunger for visual attunement and recognition in his use of regression in the service of the ego. Using projection, he was able to give expression to his inner feelings through a variety of play characters. He played with his ambivalence regarding closeness to the object (the camera) using avoidance, reaction formation (his attacks against the camera), and intellectualization. Through the medium of the video camera George experimented with the perspective from which to view and connect with this desired/threatening object. As his play strategies became more flexible, he relied less on omnipotent control and increasingly could place himself in the role of aggressor. One reminder of George's prior social isolation remained in the representation of the black hole, a void of formlessness that manifested the strategy of dedifferentiation. As he approached the terror of the black hole, George fearlessly explored the boundary between the real and the imagined.

By the end of treatment George's playfulness had advanced to new heights of hilarity and trial risk-taking. In the last play activity segment described, George directly approached his therapist with provocative, assertive moves that alternated with hidden, secretive activities. He was experimenting, in the state of playfulness, with gaining reciprocity wherein he could exchange roles, goals, thoughts, and feelings with his therapist. Who was the deceiver? Who was the deceived? Who was the victim? Who was the thief? In exchanging passive for active means of communication, George was able to express early infantile needs and wishes without the fear of retaliation or loss of relationship. Regression when it occurred was in the service of deepening the play to explore his intense needs for emotional dependence and closeness.

George made considerable use of varied adaptive strategies, including humor, anticipation, sublimation, and identification. Indications of conflict appeared in his continued use of reaction formation and projection. Doing and undoing was another conflictual strategy used to forestall fear and enable the play activity to continue. The themes of this conflictual play were greed and cannibalism, play themes that were becoming increasingly familiar to George. At first he played at being fearful of the doctor who took kids home and ate them for dinner, and later he played at consuming his own prey (the poker chips). Dispersing characters in play was George's recurrent response to being overwhelmed, perhaps a memory of early feelings and how he would create chaos in the family as a screen to hide his state of extreme anxiety. Barely disguised in pretend play dispersing (the scattering of play characters) functioned to end the play activity. In this way, the early experience of extreme anxiety previously unthinkable became transformed into a conscious representation as a play activity.

Coping/Defensive Play Strategies and the Emergence of Psychic Reality

In revisiting George's profile of coping/defensive strategies, the capacity of play to accelerate and repair development is manifest. How do these coping/defensive strategies perform this function? Mary Target and Peter Fonagy (1997) have suggested from a clinical perspective a process whereby a child develops a sense of psychic reality. According to their theoretical model, in early childhood psychic reality is characterized by two modes of relating internal experiences to the external situation. In the *psychic equivalence mode* the child expects the internal world in himself and others to correspond to external reality; in the *pretend mode* the child knows that internal experience may not reflect external reality and thinks that the internal world has no relationship to the outside world and no implications for it. Sigmund Freud's (1908) observations noted how the young child is serious about his pretend world and knows it is separate from the everyday world. Target and Fonagy commented, however, that the child's affective investment in his play may directly reflect the extent to which his fantasy incorporates a disguised piece of "serious" reality, such as the relationship between his parents or the imagined consequences of acting on dangerous wishes. In normal development the child integrates these two modes to arrive at a stage of *mentalisation*, or *reflective mode*. In the reflective mode, mental states are experienced as representations. Inner reality can then be seen as linked with external reality, yet each realm retains its distinctive qualities. Furthermore, neither realm needs to be equated with the other or split off from the other.

Reflecting on George's mental states, his therapist facilitated George's process of mentalisation. As therapy progressed, George was increasingly able to represent his ideas and feelings. This progress was possible because of the safe state of playfulness. George was able to express his feelings and wishes (when he was only pretending) and in interaction with his therapist have them recognized as existing outside of his own mind. Moreover, the therapist responded playfully by exaggerating reality, and George's pretend experience could become blended with something real.

When George was a young child, his difficult early experiences of connection and disconnection with his parents had led to a partial failure in the integration of these two modes of experiencing reality. He experienced early feelings surrounding nurturance needs within the mode of psychic equivalence; he could not move beyond experiencing these earliest wishes and fears as if they were real. The therapist's awareness of George's inner world enabled George to dare to think about his feelings and thoughts as representations, rather than replicas, of external reality.

The profile of coping/defensive strategies can be viewed as illustrating George's progress in mentalisation, that is, in integrating psychic equivalence and pretense. While his play activity became more adaptive and interactive, it remained predominantly conflictual. Moreover, his play activity strategies continued to reflect, to a minimal degree, intense anxiety and social isolation. These intense fantasies remained entrenched in the pretend mode. They were expressed through the depiction of a terrifying black hole and through the activities of dispersal and dedifferentiation. Despite this intermittent intrusion of intense anxiety, George was able to be predominantly aware of himself as playing.

Revisiting Sammy

In contrast to George's profiles, the profile of Sammy's coping/defensive strategies depicted a child who was minimally aware of his role as player. As has just been described, to the extent that a child can mediate between the realm of pretense and the realm of the real through the medium of mentalisation or representation, we can clearly observe the activity of the self. In these instances of normal development, the child himself engages in active commerce between these two realms, each of which enriches the experience of the other. When first engaged in treatment, Sammy was predominantly preoccupied within his own world of sensorimotor fantasies. His realm of pretense included soft and hard objects experienced as extensions of his own body, protecting him from external intrusions. Sammy's early history was replete with parental absence, fear, confusion, and depression. There was no one available to him to aid him in integrating his internal states with external events. Significantly, Sammy's highest levels of relating were observed in relationship to his older brother, whom he was able to both imitate and prey upon in play.

The two profiles of defensive–coping strategies provided a measure of Sammy's emergent representational capacities. The integration of his intense fantasies with interpersonal experience through the use of play strategies also enabled him to gain perspective on himself in the role of player. In the first session, Sammy demonstrated minimal problem-solving abilities in attempting to put together two tracks. He also evidenced conflict by avoiding interaction and regressing to the neediness of a much younger child. In the beginning of treatment Sammy's play style was dominated by the use of extremely anxious/isolated strategies, including constriction and dismantling.

From Sammy's profile of play it was clear that his social constriction had immediate consequences in the constriction of his experience of himself. In regressing into a general state of withdrawal, Sammy remained unconnected to the source of possible personal growth and development. In this sense Sammy created his own dilemma of unrelatedness. As if through metaphor (a hint of Sammy's potential for integration), however, Sammy showed an interest in connectedness by focusing on the task of putting railroad tracks together.

The second session analyzed manifested a very significant shift in Sammy's style of playing. In this session there was no evidence of extreme anxiety or isolation. Sammy had also become well aware of his role as player. He was able to integrate his fantasy world of trains, travel, catastrophe, and repair (pretend mode) with the interpersonal realities of relationship to form new representations. The small fireman who goes up and down the ladder was a translation of his new experience of his own capabilities within the language of play. The play space included three players, his mother, the therapist, and Sammy. It was within this triadic focus that Sammy was able to progress developmentally. Adaptive attributes observed in his play activity included anticipation, sublimation, affiliation, and altruism. Projection and doing and undoing (conflictual strategies) were present to a moderate degree. Sammy's progress was mirrored in his mother's active involvement, her anticipation of his play, her close bonds to him while playing, her altruism in giving of herself in the play, and the sublimation of her personal interests in the growth of her child.

Sammy's play activity demonstrated the emergence of imaginary play from shared meaningful interaction with his mother and therapist. In his isolated state at the beginning of therapy, Sammy's early attempts at play activity evoked confusion for him. His intermittent withdrawal from involvement with mother and therapist and his wandering off might be understood as efforts to regulate this initial feeling of disorganization. As therapy progressed, meaning emerged from the shared focus of the play activity. Sammy's earliest desire was to connect, and he expanded upon this desire to develop and grow by representing travel, movement, separation, and reunion. Most poignantly, Sammy represented in the last play activity segment the occurrence of breakdown and repair.

Robert Emde (1995) traced the beginnings of pretense and imaginative play activity to before the end of the second year. Citing Freud's observations of his 18-month-old grandson's "fort"..."da" ("gone" and "there") game (Freud 1920), Emde claimed that this game was an early form of pretense, making use of an alternative reality. Thus, upon his mother's departure Freud's grandson engaged in repeated solitary play involving the disappearance and return of a spool on a string. Moreover, not only was this play activity an active repetition of the experience of helplessness resulting from mother's separation, it also brought a sense of mastery in the return sequence that contained both relief and pleasure. The social aspects of this play activity were not immediately obvious, but Freud noted how the boy's mother encouraged her son's becoming aware of her return after a period of disappearance by hiding her face with her hands and then, to the child's joy, reappearing.

Robert Emde stressed the future orientation of this imaginative activity, emerging from the social play between mother and child. It was this future orientation that contained the adaptive element of hoping, imagining what would happen next. Thus, Sammy's mother when playing with him at peek-a-boo created an anticipation, a shared expectation of her reappearance. These shared joyous expectations constructed the atmosphere of hope and expectation that contributed to Sammy's enhanced development.

Looking forward enabled Sammy to construct a narrative linking events. His stories enabled him to hide objects without the fear of losing them and have objects break down without the fear of permanent injury. With these new understandings, Sammy gained new flexibility in his capacity to regulate his feelings and states of self-awareness. Thus, the development of Sammy's imagination did not add to his confusion; rather it gradually eliminated his confusion by enhancing his self-awareness and closeness in relationships with others. Play activity was the medium within which the development of these two important aspects of ego functioning—imagination and self-reflection—were observed.

Profiles of Play as a Measure for Observation of a Child's Development

Play activity, so essential to the welfare of children, can be both understood as an overall process and analyzed into specific parameters using the categories of the CPTI, a valuable tool for observation and shared clinical and scientific understanding. These categories tell us about the relationship between play and everyday reality, play and the child's emerging self-perceptions, and the role of play activity in the normal course of development and in psychopathology.

With the use of the CPTI, it is possible to identify patterns among variables that contribute to play activity, resulting in profiles of play activity. Why pursue this elaborate taxonomy? What value do these observed categories have in promoting our understanding of the process of change in play activity? Since the observer often has an immediate intuitive understanding of the child's play, one might ask if all of this analysis is necessary. The author's mission has been to demonstrate how these at times laborious procedures can provide clinicians and researchers with valuable new insights into various kinds of play, various kinds of players, and the process of change in play activity over time. It is intended that these profiles be understood as multidetermined in the case of each player. Do certain diagnostic groups, age groups, cultural groups also have characteristic profiles? Only extensive scientific epidemiological research can give the answers to this last question.

The term "profiles of play" has another connotation. Profiles are intended to identify patterns of organization that underlie manifest play activity. These profiles identify styles of playing. As play activity changes, it is possible to identify changes in parameters associated with these transformations. In addition, as demonstrated in this book a profile of play is multidimensional, therefore the CPTI facilitates greater detection of individual differences within the general category of play activity. Profiles of play capture the interplay of dynamics between regulatory mechanisms, progressive movement, regressive pulls, and creativity. A profile of play identifies an individual child's style of organization while playing, a way of expressing his own individuality.

References

Anthony, J. & Cohler, B. (eds) (1987) *The Invulnerable Child*. New York: Guilford Press.

Baron-Cohen, S. (1995) *Mindblind*. Cambridge, MA: MIT Press/Bradford Books.

Baron-Cohen, S. (1991) 'Precursors to a theory of mind: Understanding attention in others.' In A. Whiten (ed.) *Natural Theories of Mind: Evolution, Development and Stimulation of Everyday Mindreading*. Oxford, England: Basil Blackwell.

Baron-Cohen, S. (1989) 'Thinking about thinking: How does it develop? Critical notice.' *Journal of Child Psychology & Psychiatry 30*, 931–33.

Bates, E., Benigni, L., Bretherton, L., Camioni, L. & Votterra, V. (1979) *The Emergence of Symbols: Cognition and Communication in Infancy*. New York: Academic Press.

Beebe, B. & Lachman, F. (1988) 'The contribution of mother-infant mutual influence to the origins of self- and object representations.' *Psychoanalytical Psychology 5*, 305–57.

Beebe, B. & Stern, D. (1977) 'Engagement-disengagement in early object experiences.' In M. Freedman & S. Grand (eds) *Communicative Structures and Psychic Structures*. New York: Plenum Press.

Beren, P. (ed.) (1998) *Narcissistic Disorders in Children and Adolescents*. Northvale, NJ: Jason Aronson.

Bergman, A. (1999) *Ours, Yours, Mine: Mutuality and the Emergence of the Separate Self*. Northvale, NJ: Jason Aronson.

Bick, E. (1968) 'The experience of the skin in early object relations.' *International Journal of Psychoanalysis 49*, 484–86.

Bion, W. R. (1962) *Learning from Experience*. London: Heinemann Medical.

Bretherton, I. (1984) 'Representing the social world in symbolic play: Reality and fantasy.' In I. Bretherton (ed.) *Symbolic Play: The Development of Social Understanding*. Orlando, FL: Academic Press.

Bretherton, I. & Beeghly, M. (1982) 'Talking about internal states: The acquisition of an explicit theory of mind.' *Developmental Psychology. 18*, 906–21.

Bruner, J. (1990) *Acts of Meaning*. Cambridge, MA: Harvard University Press.

Chazan, S. (2001) 'Toward a nonverbal syntax of play therapy.' *Psychoanalytic Inquiry 21*, 3, 394–406.

Chazan, S. (2000) 'Using Children's Play Therapy Instrument (CPTI) to measure the development of play in simultaneous treatment.' *Infant Mental Health Journal 21*, 3, 211–21.

Chazan, S. (1995) *The Simultaneous Treatment of Parent and Child*. New York: Basic Books.

Chazan, S. (1981) 'Development of object permanence as a correlate of dimensions of maternal care.' *Developmental Psychology 17*, 79–81.

Chicchetti, D., Beeghly, M. & Weiss-Perry, B. (1994) 'Symbolic development in children with Down Syndrome and in children with autism.' In A. Slade & D. Wolf (eds) *Children at Play*. New York: Oxford University Press.

Corrigan, E. & Gordon, P. (1995) 'The mind as an object.' In E. Corrigan & P. Gordon (eds) *The Mind Object: Precocity and Pathology of Self-Sufficiency*. Northvale, NJ: Jason Aronson.

Dawson, G. (ed) (1989) *Autism: Nature, Diagnosis and Treatment*. New York: Guilford.

Drucker, J. (1979) 'The affective context and psychodynamics of first symbolization.' In M. Smith & M. Franklin (eds) *Symbolic Functioning in Childhood*. Hillsdale, NJ: Lawrence Erlbaum.

Dunn, J. & Dale, N. (1984) '"I a daddy": 2-year-olds' collaboration in joint pretend with sibling and with mother.' In I. Bretherton (ed.) *Symbolic Play: The Development of Social Understanding*. New York: Academic Press.

Emde, R. (1995) 'Fantasy and beyond: A current developmental perspective on Freud's "Creative Writers and Day-dreaming."' In E. Person, P. Fonagy, & S. Figueira (eds) *On Freud's "Creative Writers and Day-dreaming."* New Haven: Yale University Press.

Emde, R. (1992) 'Positive emotions for psychoanalytic theory: Surprises from infancy research and new directions.' In T. Shapiro & R. Emde (eds) *Affect: Psychoanalytic Perpectives*. Madison, CT: International Universities Press.

Emde, R. (1989a) 'Toward a psychoanalytic theory of affect: The organizational model and its propositions.' In S. Greenspan & G. Pollack (eds) *The Course of Life, Vol. I, Infancy*. Madison, CT: International Universities Press.

Emde, R. & Buchsbaum, H. (1989b) 'Toward a psychoanalytic theory of affect: Emotional development and signaling in infancy.' In S. Greenspan & G. Pollack (eds) *The Course of Life, Vol. I, Infancy*. Madison, CT: International Univsities Press.

Emde, R., Kubrick, L. & Oppenheim, D. (1997) 'Imaginative reality observed during early language development.' *International Journal of Psychoanalysis 78*, 115–33.

Emde, R. & Sorce, J. (1983) 'The rewards of infancy: emotional availability and maternal referencing.' In J. Call, E. Galenson, & R. Tyson (eds) *Frontiers of Infant Psychiatry, Vol. I*. New York: Basic Books.

Engel, S. (1999) *The Stories Children Tell: Making Sense of the Narrative of Childhood*. New York: W. H. Freeman & Co.

Erikson, E. (1977) *Toys and Reasons: Stages in the Ritualization Experience*. New York: W.W. Norton.

Erikson, E. (1972) 'Play and actuality.' In M. Piers (ed) *Play and Development*. New York: W. W. Norton.

Erikson, E. (1950) *Childhood and Society* (3rd ed.) New York: W. W. Norton, 1985.

Fein, G. (1987) 'The affective psychology of play.' In A. W. Gottfried & C. C. Brown (eds) *Play Interactions: The Contributions of Play Materials and Parental Involvement to Children's Development*. Lexington, MA: Lexington Books.

Fein, G. (1978) 'Play revisited.' In M. Lamb (ed.) *Social and Personality Development*. New York: Holt, Rinehart & Winston.

Fein, G. & Apfel, N. (1979) 'Some preliminary observations on knowing and pretending.' In N. Smith & M. Franklin (eds) *Symbolic Functioning in Childhood.* Hillsdale, NJ: Lawrence Erlbaum.

First, E. (1994) 'The leaving game, or I'll play you and you play me; the emergence of dramatic role play in 2-year-olds.' In A. Slade & D. Wolf (eds) *Children at Play.* New York: Oxford University Press.

Flavell, J. H. (1977) *Cognitive Development.* Englewood Cliffs, NJ: Prentice-Hall.

Fonagy, P. & Target, M. (1995) 'Playing with reality: I. Theory of mind and the normal development of psychic reality.' *International Journal of Psychoanalysis 77,* 2, 217–33.

Fraiberg, S. (1982) 'Pathological defenses in infancy.' *Psychoanalytic Quarterly 51,* 612–35.

Fraiberg, S. (1969) 'Libidinal object consistency and mental representation.' *Psychoanalytic Study of the Child 24,* 9–47.

Fraiberg, S. (1959) *The Magic Years.* New York: Scribner's.

Freud, A. (1965) *Normality and Pathology in Childhood.* New York: International Universities Press.

Freud, A. (1963) 'The concept of developmental lines.' *Psychoanalytic Study of the Child 18,* 245–65.

Freud, S. (1920) 'Beyond the pleasure principle.' *Standard Edition 18,* 7–64. London; Hogarth Press, 1955.

Freud, S. (1908) 'Creative writers and daydreaming.' In E. Person, P. Fonagy & S. Figuerira (eds) *On Freud's 'Creative Writers and Day-dreaming'.* New Haven, CT: Yale University Press, 1995.

Garner, B. (1998) 'Play development from birth to age four.' In D. Fromberg & D. Bergen (eds) *Play from Birth to Twelve and Beyond.* New York: Garland Publications.

Garvey, C. (1977) *Play.* Boston: Harvard University Press.

Greenberg, J. & Mitchell, S. (1983) *Object Relations in Psychoanalytic Theory.* Cambridge, MA: Harvard University Press.

Greenspan, S. (1991) *The Clinical Interview of the Child* (2nd ed.). Washington, DC: American Psychiatric Press.

Hobson, R. (1986) 'The autistic child's appraisal of expression of emotion: A further study.' *Journal of Child Psychology & Psychiatry 27,* 671–80.

Hunt, J. McV. (1965) 'Intrinsic motivation and its role in development.' In D. Levine (ed.) *Nebraska Symposium on Motivation.* Lincoln: University of Nebraska Press.

Izard, C. (1991) *The Psychology of Emotions.* New York: Plenum.

Johnson, J. (1998) 'Play development from ages four to eight.' In D. Fromberg & D. Bergen (eds) *Play from Birth to Twelve and Beyond.* New York: Garland Publications.

Kelly, K. (1970) 'A precocious child in analysis.' *Psychoanalytic Study of the Child 25,* 122–45.

Kernberg, O. (1975) *Borderline Conditions and Pathological Narcissism.* New York: Aronson.

Kernberg, P. (1994) 'Current perspectives in defense mechanisms.' *Bulletin of the Menninger Clinic 58,* 55–87.

Kernberg, P. (1989) *The Forms of Play.* Presentation at the American Academy of Child and Adolescent Psychiatry, New York, October 12, 1989.

Kernberg, P., Chazan, S. & Normandin, L. (1998) 'The Children's Play Therapy Instrument (CPTI) Description, Development and Reliability Studies.' *Journal of Psychotherapy, Practice & Research 7*, 3, 196–207.

Kernberg, P., Chazan, S. & Normandin, L. (1997) *Children's Play Therapy Instrument* (CPTI). Unpublished.

Klein, M. (1930) 'The importance of symbol formation in the development of the ego.' *Love, Guilt and Reparation and Other Works.* London: Hogarth, 1975.

Kohut, H. (1971) *The Analysis of the Self.* New York: International Universities Press.

Krystal, H. (1978) 'Self representation and the capacity for self care.' *The Annual of Psychoanalysis 6*, 209–46.

Lane, R. & Chazan, S. (1989) 'Symbols of terror: The witch/vampire, the spider, and the shark.' *Psychoanalytis Psychology 6*, 325–42.

Leslie, A. (1987) 'Pretence and representation: The origins of "theory of mind."' *Psychological Review 94*, 412–26.

Lichtenberg, J. (1989) *Psychoanalysis and Motivation.* New Jersey: Analytic Press.

Lipsett, L. (1976) 'Developmental psychology comes of age.' In L. P. Lipsett (ed.) *Developmental Psychology: The Significance of Infancy.* Hillsdale, NJ: Lawrence Erlbaum.

Mahler, M. (1972a) 'On the first three subphases of the separation-individuation process.' *International Journal of Psychoanalysis 53*, 333–38.

Mahler, M. (1972b) 'Rapprochement subphase of the separation-individuation process.' *Psychoanalytic Quarterly 41*, 487–506.

Mahler, M. (1968) *On Human Symbiosis and the Vicissitudes of Individuation.* New York: Internernational Universities Press.

Mahler, M, Pine, F., & Bergman, A. (1975) *The Psychological Birth of the Human Infant.* New York: Basic Books.

Mayes, L. & Cohen, D. (1992) 'The development of a capacity for imagination in early childhood.' *Psychoanal. Study Child 47*, 23–47.

Meltzer, D. *et al.* (1975) *Explorations in Autism.* Perth Shire: Clunie Press.

Milner, M. (1955) 'The role of illusion in symbol formation.' In *New Directions in Psychoanalysis 70*, 1, 127–40.

Moran, G. (1987) 'Some functions of play and playfulness.' *Psychoanalytic Study of the Child 42*, 11–29.

Murphy, L. & Moriarty, A. (1976) *Vulnerability, Coping and Growth.* New Haven, CT: Yale Univ. Press.

Murphy, L. (1962) *The Widening World of Childhood.* New York: Basic Books.

Nelson, K. (1989) *Narratives From the Crib.* Cambridge, MA: Harvard University Press.

Neubauer, P. (1987) 'The many meanings of play'. *Psychoanalytic Study of the Child 42*, 3–9.

Nicholich, L. (1977) 'Beyond sensorimotor intelligence: Assessment of symbolic maturity through analysis of pretend play.' *Merrill-Palmer Quarterly 28*, 89–99.

Ogden, T. (1989) *The Primitive Edge of Experience.* Northvale, NY: Jason Aronson.

Papousek, M., Papousek, H. & Harris, B. (1987) 'The emergence of play in parent-infant interrelations.' In D. Gorlitz & J. Wohlivill (eds) *Curiosity, Imagination and Play.* Hillsdale, NJ: Erlbaum.

Peller, L. (1954) 'Libidinal phases, ego development and play.' *Psychoanalytic Study of the Child 9*, 178–98.

Piaget, J. (1962) *Play, Dreams and Imitation*. New York: Norton.

Piaget, J. (1954) *The Construction of Reality in the Child*. New York: Basic Books.

Rose, G. (1972) 'Fusion states.' In P. Giovacchini (ed.) *Tactics and Techniques in Psychoanalytic Theory*. New York: Jason Aronson.

Rutter, M. (1983) 'Cognitive deficits in the pathogenesis of autism.' *Journal of Child Psychology & Psychiatry 24*, 513–32.

Rutter, M. (1978) 'Diagnosis and definition of childhood autism.' *Journal of Autism & Developmental Disorders 8*, 139–61.

Rutter, M. & Garmezy, N. (1983) 'Developmental psychopathology.' In P. Mussen (ed.) *Handbook of Child Psychology*. New York: Wiley.

Sander, L. (1983) 'Polarity, paradox and the organizing process in development.' In J. Call, E. Galenson, & R. Tyson (eds) *Frontier of Infant Psychiatry*. New York: Basic Books.

Sander, L. (1975) 'Infant and caregiving environment: Investigation and conceptualization of adaptive behavior in a system of increasing complexity.' In E. Anthony (ed.) *Explorations in Child Psychiatry*. New York: Plenum Press.

Sandler, J. (1960) 'The background of safety.' *International Journal of Psychoanalysis 38*, 391–97.

Sandler, J. & Rosenblatt, B. (1962) 'The concept of the representational world.' *Psychoanalytic Study of the Child 17*, 128–45.

Sandler, J. & Sandler, A. M. (1978) 'On the development of object relationships and affects.' *International Journal of Psychoanalysis 59*, 285–96.

Sarnoff, C. (1976) *Latency*. New York: Jason Aronson.

Schaefer, C., Gillin, K., & Sandgrund, A. (1991) *Play Diagnosis and Assessment*. New York: Wiley.

Schank, R. & Abelson, R. (1977) *Scripts, Plans, Goals and Understanding*. Hillsdale, NJ: Erlbaum.

Selman, R. (1980) *The Growth of Interpersonal Understanding: Developmental and Clinical Analyses*. New York: Academic Press.

Sigman, M. & Mundy, P. (1987) 'Symbolic processes in young autistic children.' *New Directions for Child Development 36*, 31–46.

Singer, D. & Singer, J. L. (1990) *The House of Make Believe: Children's Play and the Developing Imagination*. Cambridge, MA: Harvard University Press.

Slade, A. (1994) 'Making meaning and making believe: Their role in the clinical process.' In A. Slade & D. Wolf (eds) *Children at Play*. New York: Oxford Univ. Press.

Sorce, J. & Emde, R. (1981) 'Mother's presence is not enough: Effect of emotional availability on infant exploration.' *Developmental Psychology 17*, 737–45.

Stern, D. (1992) 'Pre-narrative envelope: An alternative view of "unconscious fantasy" in infancy.' *Bulletin of the Anna Freud Centre 15*, 291–318.

Stern, D. (1990) 'Joy and satisfaction in infancy.' In R. Glick & S. Bone (eds) *Pleasure Beyond the Pleasure Principle*. New Haven: Yale University Press.

Stern, D. (1985) *The Interpersonal World of the Infant*. New York: Basic Books.

Stern, D. (1977) *The First Relationship: Mother and Infant.* Cambridge, MA: Harvard University Press.

Stern, D. (1974) 'Mother and infancy at play: The dyadic interaction involving facial, vocal and gaze behaviors.' In M. Lewis & L. Rosenblum (eds) *The Effect of the Infant on Its Caregivers.* New York: Wiley.

Sutton-Smith, B. (1976) *Play and Learning.* New York: Gardner Press.

Singer, D. & Singer, J. (1990) *The House of Make-Believe: Children's Play and the Developing Imagination.* Cambridge, MA: Harvard Univ. Press.

Target, M. & Fonagy, P. (1997) 'Playing with reality: II. The development of psychic reality from a theoretical perspective.' *International Journal of Psychoanalysis 78*, 459–79.

Trad, P. (1993) 'Previewing.' *Journal of Clinical Psychol.ogy 49*, 261–77.

Trevarthen, C. (1980) 'The foundations of intersubjectivity: Development of interpersonal and cooperative understanding in infants.' In D. Olson (ed.) *The Social Foundations of Language and Thought: Essays in Honor of Jerome Bruner.* New York: W. W. Norton.

Tustin, F. (1990) *The Protective Shell in Children and Adults.* London: Karnac Books.

Tustin, F. (1972) *Autism and Childhood Psychosis.* London: Hogarth Press.

Tyson, P. & Tyson, R. (1990) *Psychoanalytic Theories of Development.* New Haven: Yale University Press.

Urist, J. (1977) 'The Rorschach Test and the assessment of object relations.' *Journal of Personality Assessment 41*, 3–9.

Vela, R., Gottlieb, E. & Gottlieb, H. (1983) 'Borderline syndromes in childhood: A critical review.' In K. Robson (ed.) *The Borderline Child.* New York: McGraw-Hill.

Vygotsky, L. (1966) 'Play and its role in the mental development of the child.' *Soviet Psychology 12*, 62–7.

Weinenger, O. (1989) 'Introduction to "What Autism Is and What Autism Is Not."' *Melanie Klein and Object-Relations 7*, 12–13.

Wellman, H. (1990) *The Child's Theory of Mind.* Cambridge, MA: MIT Press.

White, R. (1959) 'Motivation reconsidered: The concept of competence.' *Psychology Review 66*, 297–333.

Winnicott, D. (1971) *Playing and Reality.* New York: Basic Books.

Winnicott, D. W. (1963) 'From dependence towards independence in the development of the individual.' In D. W. Winnicott (ed.) *The Maturational Processes and the Facilitating Environment.* New York: International University Press, 1965.

Winnicott, D. W. (1958) 'The capacity to be alone.' In D. W. Winnicott (ed.) *The Maturational Processes and the Facilitating Environment.* New York: International University Press, 1965.

Wolf, D., Rayne, J., & Altshuler, J. (1984) 'Agency and experience: Actions and states in play narrations.' In I. Bretherton (ed.) *Symbolic Play: The Development of Social Understanding.* Orlando, FL: Academic Press.

Youngblade, L. & Dunn, J. (1995) 'Social pretend with mother and sibling: Individual differences and social understanding.' In A. Pelligrini (ed.) *The Future of Play Theory.* New York: SUNY Press.

Name index

Subject index